OUT OF THE CROCODILE

A Play in Two Acts

by

GILES COOPER

LONDON
EVANS BROTHERS LIMITED

Copyright © 1964 by Giles Cooper
All Rights Reserved

OUT OF THE CROCODILE is fully protected under the copyright laws of the British Commonwealth, including Canada, the United States of America, and all other countries of the Copyright Union. All rights, including professional and amateur stage productions, recitation, lecturing, public reading, motion picture, radio broadcasting, television and the rights of translation into foreign languages are strictly reserved.

ISBN 978-0-573-11684-1

www.samuelfrench.co.uk
www.samuelfrench.com

For Amateur Production Enquiries

United Kingdom and World excluding north america

plays@samuelfrench.co.uk

020 7255 4302/01

Each title is subject to availability from Samuel French, depending upon country of performance.

CAUTION: Professional and amateur producers are hereby warned that OUT OF THE CROCODILE is subject to a licensing fee. Publication of this play does not imply availability for performance. Both amateurs and professionals considering a production are strongly advised to apply to the appropriate agent before starting rehearsals, advertising, or booking a theatre. A licensing fee must be paid whether the title is presented for charity or gain and whether or not admission is charged.

The professional rights in this play are controlled by Samuel French Ltd (A Concord Theatricals Company), Aldwych House, 71-91 Aldwych, London, WC2B 4HN.

No one shall make any changes in this title for the purpose of production. No part of this book may be reproduced, stored in a retrieval system, or transmitted in any form, by any means, now known or yet to be invented, including mechanical, electronic, photocopying, recording, videotaping, or otherwise, without the prior written permission of the publisher. No one shall upload this title, or part of this title, to any social media websites.

The right of Giles Cooper to be identified as author of this work has been asserted in accordance with Section 77 of the Copyright, Designs and Patents Act 1988.

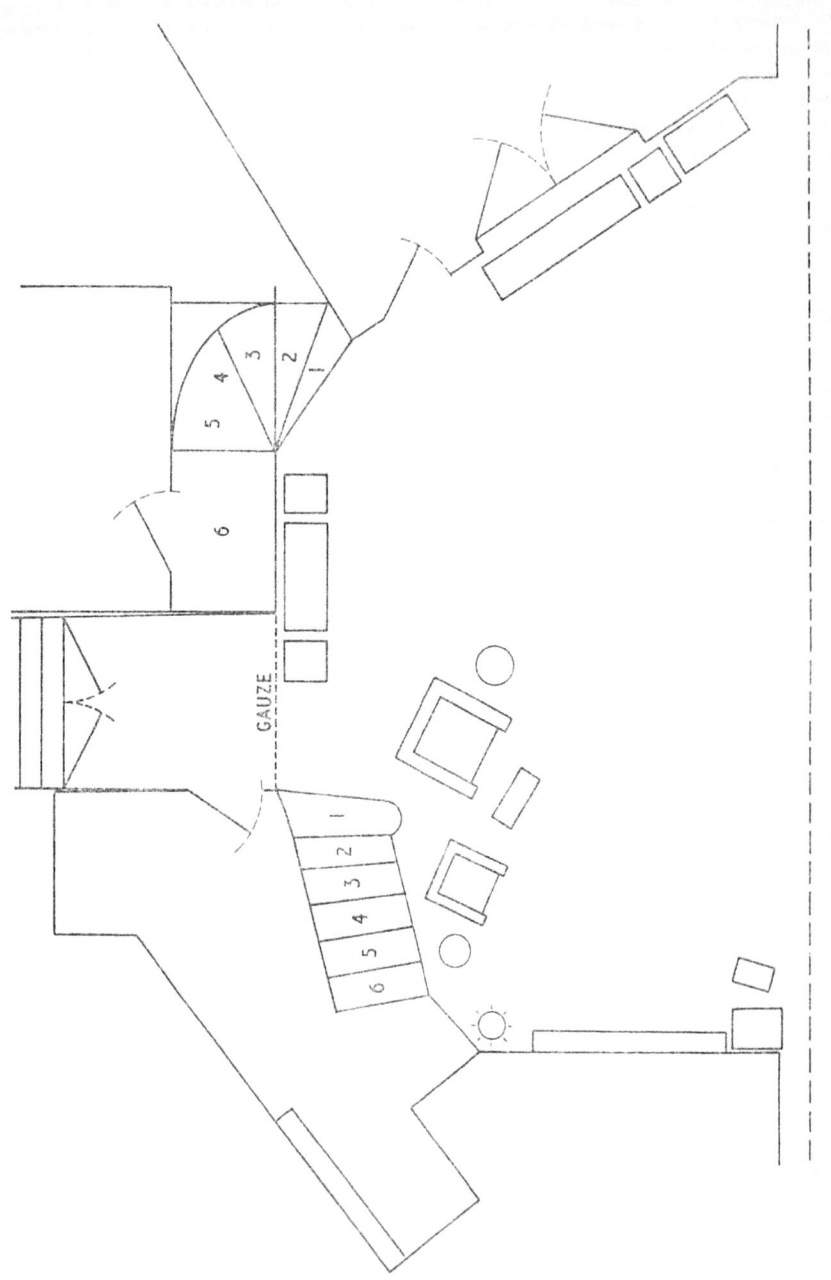

Out of the Crocodile

This play was first produced at the Phoenix Theatre, London, on 29th October 1963, with the following cast:

HENRY HAMPSTER	Cyril Raymond
HELEN HAMPSTER	Celia Johnson
PETER POUNCE	Kenneth More
MONICA	Katharine Barker
JULIA	Amanda Reiss

The play was directed by DONALD MCWHINNIE
with décor by REECE PEMBERTON

Scene: *The Hampsters' flat in London*
Time: *The present*

ACT ONE
SCENE 1 .. A morning in early summer
SCENE 2 .. A few hours later

ACT TWO
SCENE 1 .. Immediately after the previous scene
SCENE 2 .. The next morning

No reference is intended in this play to any person, alive or dead

Running time of this play, excluding intervals, is approximately one hour and forty-five minutes.

AUTHOR'S NOTE

This play is mainly about the danger of not looking round from time to time to see where we have been, and where we are going.

The Hampsters, while never content with each other, are totally content with themselves. It takes them a long time to appreciate the existence of a new situation, and a longer time to adapt themselves to it. Provided that they are given the time, they can survive, but if hurried they will only make self-destructive attempts to turn matters to their own immediate advantage.

It would, however, be a great mistake to approach this play too seriously. Every laugh is legitimate, but it should be remembered from time to time that in its cold reptilian heart the Crocodile is less than amiable. It has teeth and it is always hungry. It will defend itself at the first hint of attack, and being extremely wily will suddenly appear, jaws agape, just at the moment when it seems to have been evaded.

In plain terms this means that producers and actors must not be afraid of checking the audience's laughter when necessary, although they must recapture it again as quickly as possible.

The device by which we see the characters arrive outside the door of the flat is not absolutely essential. It has considerable advantages in the first act, and helps to set the style for the play, which is not entirely naturalistic, but in the second act it has the disadvantage that when Julia arrives and knocks on the door we know who it is, and so we do not join the Hampsters in their sudden realization that everything is over. On balance I am inclined to think that we lose more than we gain by seeing into the hall, particularly as the device can only be convincing on a really deep stage. GILES COOPER

PRODUCTION NOTE

The play is technically quite simple to stage (see Author's Note on the set). Most of the moves and positions have been left to the producer's discretion, but, working on a simplified version of the plan and photo supplied, these should more or less fall into place.

Lighting is straightforward in the main. A subtle, and discreet, change might occur on Peter's first entry. The only cues which may present problems occur towards the end of Act One, Scene Two. The fade referred to just before the close should start some minutes earlier—or could be omitted if the curtains are presumed to shut out all exterior light. The glow from the television set can be worked by a dimmer wired to the bulb inside the supposed cabinet (which should, of course, face well upstage), and the flicker should not be too distracting. Care should be taken to reproduce as closely as possible the blue-grey light from a television screen. A good effect can be obtained by using a double "steel-blue" gelatine.

The dialogue, brilliantly (and very amusingly) naturalistic even when the fantastic takes over, and often in sequences of very brief lines, needs handling crisply, quick on cues, but without the pace overreaching itself into a gabble.

The cast is made up of five characters—a middle-aged couple, a young (or youngish) man, and two contrasted girls, all very rewarding parts. The Hampsters themselves afford opportunities for high comedy playing—at first apparently altogether conventional, until the surfaces crack to reveal a somewhat uncomfortable parable about what *might* happen (though not, unfortunately, so entertainingly) to any of us. The mysterious, outwardly charming, Peter Pounce has been aptly described as an anti-hero, and to the end we are not quite sure of him. Is there somewhere a hint of Puck—or even of the cloven hoof?

It is an original, diverting, very amusing—and at the same time slightly sinister play to present, the author driving home his uncomfortable message with both force and humour.
IVAN BUTLER

N.B.–Interleaved producer's copies of this play are available, price 10s. 6d. (postage 7d. extra), *direct from the publishers only.*

*OUT OF THE CROCODILE

ACT ONE

SCENE I

The flat is comfortable, but it seems to have been lived in for a very long time. Everything is a little worn and drab. It is a fine day in early summer and the window on the small balcony is open. HENRY *and* HELEN *are in the middle of a furious row, neither listening to the other, both talking at the same time.*

HENRY. Sixty-three, sixty-three, sixty-three!
HELEN. Sixty-five, I know it's sixty-five! Why won't you listen to me? I keep telling you it's sixty-five.
HENRY. Sixty-three, sixty-three—you are the most obstinate woman I've ever met.
HELEN. Do you think I've no education at all? Do you think I can't add, multiply, divide? What do you think I am?
HENRY. Quite wrong, totally wrong. I can do logarithms and it's sixty-three.
 (There is a pause.)
HELEN. Obstinate.
HENRY *(calm and dignified).* Correct that's all, just correct.
HELEN. If you won't admit it, then you won't. *(She picks up a suitcase off the floor and takes it off to the bedroom* R.*)*
HENRY. I'll show you a very simple practical demonstration; matches. *(He takes a box off the mantelpiece and another from his pocket.)* If you can count I will make it absolutely clear that seven nines are sixty-three. *(He clears a space on the table and empties out the matches.)* You'll have to admit it when it's in front of your eyes. *(He starts counting out the matches in rows.)* One, two, three, four, five, six, seven—seven ones and one, two, three, four, five, six, seven—is seven twos.
HELEN *(off).* Twice seven, not seven twos.
HENRY. Or two times seven, or seven times two, it's all the same. Here's three times seven.
 *(*HELEN *re-enters.)*
HELEN. Twice seven is what they say in educated schools.
HENRY. Educated schools, what an expression! Does nothing mean

*It is illegal to perform this play, *in any circumstances whatsoever*, without a licence. Please refer, for full details, to Copyright Notice on page 2 of cover. *(Copyright Act 1956.)*

anything to you? Five sevens—I need more matches. (*He finds some book matches in his pocket and starts pulling them out one by one.*)

HELEN. What are you doing?

HENRY (*timing his words to the putting down of the matches*). Making you see that I know what I'm talking about. Look, seven sevens, you can't deny that, can you?

HELEN. I'm not interested; it's nothing at all to me.

HENRY. Seven eights are fifty-six and seven nines—

HELEN. Are sixty-five.

HENRY. Oh yes? (*He has now got the matches in order, rank by rank. He straightens one or two meticulously and steps back.*) Count them.

(HELEN *is putting a cigarette into her mouth.*)

HELEN. Give me a match.

HENRY. Count them, count them, count them!

HELEN. Don't fly into a rage.

HENRY. I'm not in a rage; I'm perfectly calm. I simply, simply, simply want you to count these matches.

(HELEN *gives a light amused shrug as if to say "The children must be humoured", then crosses to the table.* HENRY *stands back, arms folded, a smirk of expectant triumph on his face.*)

HELEN. Count them all?

HENRY. All.

(HELEN's *lips move as she starts to count.* HENRY *rocks on his heels.* HELEN *comes to the end. There is a pause.*)

Well?

HELEN. Forty-two.

HENRY. Nonsense.

HELEN. I make it forty-two.

HENRY. Then you can't even count. How dare you say I can't multiply —you can't add! Look: one, two, three, four, five, six, seven, and another seven, fourteen, and another, twenty-one, and another, twenty-eight, and again, thirty-five—and again, forty-two, forty-nine—

HELEN (*checking him*). Ah!

HENRY. What's the matter?

HELEN. Book matches count half. (*She picks one up, strikes it and lights her cigarette.*) It's obvious. Look at them. You can't count them the same as ordinary ones.

HENRY. But they aren't matches!

HELEN. Dearest, I don't think you're well. Look at them.

HENRY. They're objects, things, digits!

HELEN (*blankly*). Digits!

HENRY. They might be anything.

(HELEN *starts putting the matches back into a box.*)

SCENE I] OUT OF THE CROCODILE 7

HELEN. But they happen to be matches.
HENRY. You are, without exception, the most pig-headed, ill-educated half-wit of a woman that I have ever known. You always have been —yes, and you always will be—yes, because you're too stupid to know what a fool you are.
  (HELEN *looks at him dumbly, outraged. She sits in an armchair and picks up her knitting.* HENRY *puts the remaining matches back in the box in silence. He is not quite sure what to do with the book matches, so he puts them in an ashtray. Finally he speaks.*)
Twelve-thirty.
  (*No answer.*)
We'd better be off.
  (*No answer.*)
You know how the road gets. (*He picks up his suitcase.*) Where's the bag?
HELEN (*indicating the bedroom*). In there.
HENRY. We'll never get to Brighton at this rate.
HELEN. I'm not going to Brighton.
HENRY. We must go to Brighton.
HELEN. I'm staying here.
HENRY. But we never spend the week-end here, we never have.
HELEN. I'm staying.
HENRY. We've a flat at Brighton; we live there—well, at week-ends.
HELEN. You go.
HENRY. Yes, of course, but we really must be leaving.
HELEN. You go, I stay.
  (HENRY *puts down the bag.*)
HENRY. I go, you stay?
  (HELEN *nods and knits.*)
That would mean I was there and you were here. Oh no, that would never do.
HELEN. I refuse to go to Brighton with a man who insults me.
HENRY. I'm not a man; I'm me, your husband.
HELEN. You insulted me to my face.
HENRY. Oh, do stop knitting!
  (HELEN *obediently puts her knitting down.*)
Come along, let's go.
  (*He picks up the bag.* HELEN *shakes her head.*)
HELEN. I told you. You will not listen when I tell you, but I told you.
HENRY. Helen, this is something we simply don't do.
HELEN. No, it's something we haven't done; now I'm doing it.
HENRY. You're not doing anything, you're just sitting there.
HELEN. And you're going to Brighton.
HENRY. Then we'd be separated.

HELEN (*after a moment's thought*). Yes.
HENRY. But we're man and wife.
HELEN. What?
HENRY. Married, have been for years; it's our tin wedding or something next week.
HELEN. Thursday, but I'm not going to Brighton.
HENRY. All because of a stupid argument about the multiplication table.
HELEN. I'm glad you see it was stupid.
HENRY. My bit of it wasn't, my bit was perfectly sensible and absolutely right.
HELEN. Oh, not again; don't keep on about it. (*She rises and goes towards the bedroom.*) The clean towel is in the airing cupboard; don't wipe your razor on it. (*She goes out.*)
HENRY. I'm not going if you're not going.
HELEN (*off*). Someone has to. Mrs. Piggott will have opened the windows. Who's going to shut them if it rains?
HENRY. I could send her a telegram, 'Go and shut windows if rain'—no, 'If look like rain shut windows'.
   (*He goes towards the telephone.* HELEN *comes to the bedroom door.*)
HELEN. She won't know what windows.
HENRY. 'If look like rain shut our windows Hampster', or 'Shut Hampster windows if rain likely Hampster'—that would do.
HELEN. We don't know her address.
   (HENRY *paces up and down restlessly. He looks at* HELEN.)
HENRY. Do you want me to go?
HELEN. Yes.
HENRY. For the week-end?
HELEN. Yes.
HENRY. Why?
HELEN. Because you're rude.
HENRY. Oh, now look here, you're behaving like a child. This is absurd; we're adults, we can't behave like this. I don't say I'm perfect, but I do my best; you've never complained before. I really don't know what's got into you.
   (*In the middle of this speech* HELEN *walks to* HENRY's *bag, which is in the centre of the stage, picks it up, goes to the balcony and drops it out. She then returns to the chair and picks up her knitting.* HENRY *looks at her in utter disbelief. He goes to the balcony and looks down.*)
And what do you think will have happened to my after-shave?
HELEN. Go down and see.
HENRY. If I do I shan't come back.
HELEN. I don't care.
HENRY. Then I'll go. (*Pause.*) Well?

HELEN. Go.
    (*She shrugs slightly and sits.* HENRY *goes to the door and opens it. He is about to make some final dramatic pronouncement, but cannot think of one. He mutters to her instead.*)
HENRY. Don't leave all the lights on. I'll be using some, too.
    (*He goes.* HELEN *stretches, puts her feet up on a stool and looks around the room. Reaching out to a table beside her she puts on, quite unnecessarily, a table lamp. Outside, a car can be heard starting up. She goes out quickly to the balcony, where she almost calls out and then decides not to. She comes back into the room and stands in the middle of it. She picks up a book, looks at it and puts it down. She then moves over to a record player in the corner and takes out a record, but before she can put it on she catches sight of herself in the mirror. She looks at herself with interest, steps back for a long view, turns round and looks over her shoulder—not really satisfactory. She knows what to do.*)
HELEN. I know—I know—
    (*She goes into the bedroom. A key is heard in the front door and* PETER POUNCE *enters carrying a zip-bag. He stands for a moment looking round. Makes a slight exclamation of satisfaction and turning to the mantelpiece he starts to take down the picture which hangs over it. At this moment* HELEN *reappears from the bedroom carrying a cheval glass. She sees* PETER *and sets it down.*)
    What are you doing?
PETER (*absently*). I live here.
HELEN. You do no such thing.
    (PETER *has got the picture in both hands and lifted it off the wall. He now turns and sees* HELEN.)
PETER. Good God!
HELEN. Put that picture back at once; I'll call the police. (*She moves towards the telephone.*)
PETER. I shouldn't do that.
HELEN. Who are you?
PETER. The name is Peter Pounce, and you're supposed to be in Brighton.
HELEN. You've been watching our movements.
PETER. Not for years.
HELEN. You have, of course you have. You saw the car drive off and you came in to steal things.
PETER (*indicating picture*). Who'd steal that?
HELEN. You've taken it down.
PETER (*pointing to another picture across the room*). I usually have those two boats over the mantelpiece.
HELEN. Usually?
PETER. Always.

HELEN. Always when?
PETER. When I come here.
HELEN. You've been here before?
PETER. I live here.
HELEN. No, some other flat.
PETER. With the same pictures? Don't be silly.
HELEN. But we live here, my husband and me.
PETER. During the week.
HELEN. All the time.
PETER. No, no, you go to Brighton at week-ends.
HELEN. And do you mean to say—
PETER. Yes, I do.
HELEN. To say that you—
PETER. Yes.
HELEN. That you come here when we go.
PETER. I do.
HELEN. While we're in Brighton you're here?
PETER. That's right.
HELEN. Every single week-end you sneak in and occupy our flat?
PETER. No more than you sneak in every Monday morning as soon as I've gone. (*He crosses to the other picture and takes it off its hook.*)
HELEN. But this is our place, my flat. Will you leave the pictures alone!
PETER. I like things to be right.
      (HELEN *rushes at him and kicks him on the shin.* PETER *clutches it with an exclamation of pain.*)
HELEN. Now get out before I ring the police.
      (PETER *sits in a chair, rubbing his shin.*)
PETER. That hurt.
HELEN. I meant it to. (*She goes to the telephone and picks up the receiver.*)
PETER. It'll cost you two years' rent at ten guineas a week.
      (HELEN *dials nine nine nine.*)
HELEN. I don't care—what did you say?
PETER. Two years' rent. At ten guineas a week.
HELEN. How do you know our rent?
PETER. It's the sort of thing you want to know about your home.
HELEN. My home.
PETER. Our home. (*He rises and hobbles towards the picture.*) How you do kick.
      (HELEN *hears a sound from the receiver.*)
HELEN. Oh—
PETER. One thousand and forty guineas.
      (HELEN *looks uncertainly at the receiver.* PETER *takes it from her and speaks into it.*)
I'm sorry, it was a mistake. (*He replaces the receiver.*)

HELEN. There was no mistake.
PETER. It won't help to fill the place with firemen. (*He picks up the second picture and takes it across to the fireplace.*) I put a new wire on this one last week-end, the old one was worn. We don't want a death in the family. (*He hangs up the picture and picks up the other one.*)
HELEN. And what am I supposed to do?
PETER. You're supposed to be in Brighton. Have you had a row with your husband?
HELEN. Yes.
PETER. The best thing would be to go down there and make it up, but do go ahead and have a look at yourself from behind first.
HELEN. That wasn't what I was doing at all.
PETER. Yes, it was. (*He goes to the cheval glass and moves it.*) You were going to put this here—no, about there, and then you were going to stand between it and the other one and see how you looked from behind.
HELEN. I was not!
PETER (*standing between the two mirrors*). Sideways then, it's the same idea. Here, this is the place.
HELEN. Anything I was doing or anything I have done is absolutely no business of yours.
(*He takes hold of her and moves her to the spot.*)
PETER. There, that's what other people see.
HELEN. I don't care.
(PETER *moves the long mirror slightly.*)
PETER. Now for the man behind you on the escalator.
HELEN (*indicating with her hand*). A bit more.
PETER. That?
HELEN. Yes, and why shouldn't I?
PETER. No reason, but you wouldn't do it in front of Henry.
HELEN. Do you know my husband?
PETER. As well as I know you. (*He holds the mirror.*) I'll put this back; it's interesting, but one soon gets tired of it. (*He takes the mirror into the bedroom.*)
HELEN. Come out of my bedroom!
PETER (*off*). Mine till Monday. Yours is in Brighton. (*He re-enters.*)
HELEN. My God, I do dislike you.
PETER. I'm no trouble.
HELEN. But you're here.
PETER. Oh yes, I'm here. (*He hangs up the first picture in the place of the second.*) I don't like it there any more than over the mantelpiece, but one doesn't have to look at it so often.
HELEN. Thank you.
PETER. It's better than those china dogs at Brighton.

HELEN. They're Staffordshire, my grandmother left them to me— (*Suddenly realizing.*) Brighton? You know our flat at Brighton?
PETER. Where do you think I spend the week?
HELEN. You mean that when we're up here, you're down there?
PETER. And the other way round, yes. (*He is now unpacking his bag, taking out various foodstuffs.*)
HELEN. It's criminal.
PETER. Name the crime.
HELEN. Breaking and entering.
PETER. I have a key.
HELEN. False pretences.
PETER. I've been perfectly frank with you.
HELEN. But not when we didn't know about you.
PETER. I was perfectly frank with myself then. (*He picks up the food and moves toward the kitchen door.*) I told myself that if you did know, there would be a lot of argument that would get us nowhere. (*He goes out into the kitchen.*)
HELEN. There will be no argument and it will get you into the street, where you belong.
PETER (*off*). Oh, I shouldn't think so.
HELEN (*yelling*). Come out of my kitchen!

(PETER *appears in the doorway.*)

PETER. What?
HELEN. My kitchen, come out of it.

(PETER *goes across to the suitcase, from which he takes a box of cigarettes.*)

PETER. You hate your kitchen.
HELEN. I do not.
PETER (*starting to fill a silver cigarette-box on the table*). The dishmop, the sink tidy and the oven cloth all echo with your sighs when you're not there. Even the old soap saucer on the window-sill. "Why do I slave away for this oaf?"
HELEN. Henry is not an oaf.
PETER. He is when you're in the kitchen and he's sitting in front of the fire trying to clean his pipe with your nail scissors. Ten cigarettes of yours, fifty of mine, have one.

(*She takes one.*)

HELEN. Oh—!
PETER. Yes?
HELEN. Nothing.
PETER (*lighting her cigarette*). You've just realized why you always seem to come back to more cigarettes than you left behind. You see, you can't accuse me of theft.

HELEN. I can accuse you of something; of course I can. I must be able to. Stealing food.
PETER. I bring my own and leave what I don't eat.
HELEN. Using things then. Dirtying sheets, wearing our carpets.
PETER. I keep the place aired.
HELEN. What about Mrs. Piggott? Is she in it with you?
PETER. As a matter of fact, I am Mrs. Piggott.
HELEN. Her son!
PETER. No, I'm her. Just think for a moment, how long since you saw her?
HELEN. Some months.
PETER. Nearly two years.
HELEN. I left her messages and money.
PETER. I know, "Please dust under bed, new paper on larder shelves, scrub both."
HELEN. Bath.
PETER. Oh, was that it? You should write better. It's all right, though; the bath wasn't too bad.
HELEN. Look, are you telling me that all the things Mrs. Piggott is supposed to do, you do?
PETER. That's right; she sacked herself soon after I arrived. Just as well. She used to pinch your butter.
HELEN. And the money, two pounds a week?
PETER. I did the job.
HELEN. That's theft.
PETER. You've never complained.
HELEN. We left her a box of chocolates at Christmas!
PETER. Someone gave them to you; they were lying around here the week-end before. Hard centres; I suppose your teeth can't manage them. They cost me a stopping.
HELEN. They were not intended for you and you ate them; that's stealing.
PETER. You may be right.
HELEN. I know I'm right, and so will the police and so will the judge.
PETER. Magistrate; it wouldn't go before a judge.
HELEN. Living on somebody else for two years certainly will.
PETER. You've got to be more specific. There's nothing but the chocolates to be specific about, and after all you'd have been terribly offended if I'd left them.
HELEN. I don't know what to think or what to do; I wish you'd go away.
PETER. I can't possibly do that. I've someone coming to lunch.
HELEN (*jolted*). You've what? Who?
PETER. A guest.

HELEN. You entertain here?
PETER. I have to entertain somewhere.
HELEN. As far as I am concerned you don't have to do anything anywhere; it's bad enough that you're here without your friends turning the place into a bear-garden.
PETER. There is no such thing.
HELEN. Oh yes, there is; it's what young men turn anywhere into.
PETER. I don't entertain young men.
HELEN. Girls?
PETER. Yes.
HELEN. You have girls up here?
PETER. Yes.
HELEN. Girls in my flat!
PETER. And your husband's.
HELEN. Not yours at any rate, and you—you, a complete stranger, calmly turn it into a kind of brothel every Saturday.
PETER. What I do is done entirely for your sake, so please moderate your language.
HELEN. I beg your pardon?
PETER. Entirely for your sake. These girls are very nice, proper, respectable girls in responsible positions. The one who's coming to lunch happens to be your landlord.
HELEN. Rubbish, our landlord's an insurance company.
PETER. Not according to the Pounce Theory.
HELEN. The what?
PETER. The Pounce Theory of Ultimate Responsibility.
HELEN. I'm not interested in your theories.
PETER. You are in this one. Have you ever been to your landlord's offices?
HELEN. No.
PETER. Well, they're in a kind of cathedral in Finsbury and I suppose somewhere in there is a chap whose job it is to collect the rents.
HELEN. Of course.
PETER. Now, if you were late with your rent, what do you suppose would happen?
HELEN. He'd write to us.
PETER. Ah, there you are one hundred per cent wrong. The Hampster fallacy demonstrated. What he would do would be to dictate a letter to a girl.
HELEN. I suppose so.
PETER. And the girl would type it out and take it back to him for signature; he would write his name on it and give it back to her. She would then lick it up and send it to you. All right?
HELEN. All right, but pointless.

PETER. Don't you realize that in the course of this operation all but one of the actions have been taken by this girl?
HELEN. Who is she?
PETER. That doesn't matter, that's not the point, at least it does matter and it is the point, but I'm not ready for it yet. The real point is that the girl is far more your landlord than X in his office and ten times more your landlord than a limited company can ever be. Now do you see what this theory is?
HELEN. No.
PETER. That the world is run by girls. When your bank manager writes to you to say that you've no more money, all the work is done by a girl.
HELEN. But a machine adds up the money.
PETER. Worked by a girl. Ditto for the Inland Revenue, your butcher, your baker, your fishmonger, the rating officer, the Electricity Board and the North Thames Gas.
HELEN. All girls?
PETER. Fat girls, thin girls, spotty girls, pale girls, but all most certainly girls. They control the world.
HELEN. Well?
PETER. All one has to do to control one's destiny is to get hold of these girls.
HELEN. And do what?
PETER. Stop them sending letters to you! After all, they don't want to; they'd much rather throw you into the wastepaper basket and lose you. All one has to do then is to make sure you stay lost.
HELEN. Not a word do I believe, you're simply making excuses for your disgusting behaviour.
PETER (*who has begun to lay the table for two*). There is no disgusting behaviour; there is very careful behaviour.
HELEN. Oh, don't be silly; it's quite obvious that you're using our flat to seduce young women in.
PETER. That would be absolutely fatal.
   (*He takes a silver salt-cellar from the cupboard.*)
HELEN. We don't use that salt-cellar.
PETER. I do. Only the best is good enough for your landlord. I can't tell you how wrong you are; seduction would be disastrous. Once you start that sort of thing you have to go on. Besides, there are far too many. Your landlord for lunch, the gas to tea and your bank manager this evening. What do you think I am? (*He stands looking at the table.*) French mustard.
   (HELEN *moves towards the kitchen, then stops.*)
HELEN. You are not going to eat our mustard.
PETER. No, I don't like it. Monica may.

HELEN. Don't you know?
PETER. I've only met her once, last week-end. She's taken over from a girl called Alison. Just as well, Alison was fond of travel. She wanted to give me a bicycle. Of course, it means a lot of work has to be done on Monica.
HELEN. Oh, yes?
PETER. I haven't really established myself as a character.
HELEN. I wouldn't have thought that would have taken you any time at all.
PETER. Heavens, yes! First of all you've got to decide what you're going to be a character in.
HELEN. In my flat, as far as I can see.
PETER. No, no, no, you don't understand. I'm not trying to be a real character.
HELEN. What then?
PETER. A figment.
HELEN (*blankly*). Figment—
PETER. Of the imagination. All these girls lead two lives; one of them is deadly dull; up in the morning, rush hour, the office, home in the evening, day in and day out: awful. That's the life in which they write letters to you asking for money. My technique is to become part of their other lives in which they see themselves as characters in films or novels or television plays, any kind of fiction.
HELEN. They must know perfectly well what you are.
PETER. They know perfectly well what they are, but it doesn't stop them wishing that someone had made them up and put them into a play with everything leading to a happy-ever-after ending.
HELEN. What happens when they find out there isn't a happy ending?
PETER. They don't; we stay on the same page all the time—somewhere around the middle.
HELEN. Don't they get bored?
PETER. No, they like it; it makes them feel safe as well as glamorous. They'd do anything rather than break the illusion, so they lose me in the files. (*He looks at the table appraisingly.*) Of course, one's got to strike the right note; no use handing them the wrong kind of fiction or they won't believe in it. This girl reads women's magazines. (*He goes to the window and lets down a sunblind.*) That's better: lucky you had these otherwise it would have had to be an evening party, "Candle-light on gleaming silver" and all that nonsense. As it is we can have a simple lettuce-crisp lunch in cool and gracious surroundings. (*He takes a bottle of hock from his bag and hands it to her.*) In the fridge, please; not too high up.

(HELEN *takes the bottle and goes out obediently.* PETER *realizes that she has done so. An idea strikes him. He nods to himself and takes a*

couple of glasses from the cupboard. From the kitchen comes a loud electrical whine.)
What's that?
(HELEN *reappears.*)
HELEN. What?
PETER. That.
(HELEN *pops back into the kitchen. The whine ceases. She returns.*)
HELEN. What?
PETER. What was it?
HELEN. It's our Eliminator. It's marvellous. It chews up all our rubbish and washes it away down the drain. They only installed it on Wednesday. Come and have a look at it.
PETER. No time now. You should have opened that bottle.
HELEN. I'm not going to be treated like a servant in my own house.
PETER. I was wondering about that. What are you going to be?
HELEN. Nothing.
PETER. You're going to Brighton?
HELEN. I am going to stay here in my flat.
PETER. Then you won't be nothing, you'll be very much something, but what?
HELEN. Me.
PETER. Let's run it over. (*He mimes an introduction.*) Monica, this is Mrs. Hampster, who actually owns this flat; she's supposed to be down at Brighton, but she had a row with her husband. I only live here when she's away. No, it won't do; it isn't romantic. First thing on Monday morning a Hampster file will move from the bottom of the filing cabinet to the boss's desk. "Take a letter, Miss Parsons", and that one won't disappear, oh no, no, no. That'll come popping through your letter-box on Tuesday morning, closely followed I don't doubt by a man in a bowler hat.
HELEN. But is it true? Is it really true?
PETER. That you pay no rent? Oh yes. You've been at the bottom of that cabinet for two solid years.
HELEN. All because of you and this girl?
PETER. Her predecessor. Nobody can possibly send landlord's letters to someone they know. In the case of the others, of course, it's mostly bills that lie around until the mice eat them.
HELEN. You've practically made us into criminals.
PETER. Didn't you realize that you hadn't paid?
HELEN. My husband deals with bills.
PETER. Then you'd better talk it over with him.
HELEN. I most certainly will.
PETER. Very unwise to do anything hasty before you have.
HELEN. But what can I do?

O.C.–B

PETER. Let's think; we need a romantic situation; you wouldn't like to be the poor mad creature I married?
HELEN. No, I would not.
PETER. I'd lock you in the bedroom and every now and then you'd give a hideous laugh, no?
HELEN. No.
            (PETER *walks up and down, thinking*.)
PETER. My mother—no. My secretary—no, that wouldn't do. I know: family retainer. When the estate came under the hammer, after my father's death in the hunting field, you said: "Master Peter needs me, I'd rather serve true blood for a pittance than be a lackey to the newly rich." I wonder what you were—the old housekeeper?
HELEN. I'm not old.
PETER. You will be to Monica. No, I think you were the head parlourmaid, very superior, rather austere, known by your surname.
HELEN. Hampster?
PETER. Oh no, I'm Hampster. It's important that I should be. What's your maiden name?
HELEN. I was Farthingale.
PETER. Once a Farthingale always a Farthingale.
HELEN. I'm not acquiescing.
PETER. No, no.
HELEN. I mean, it's outrageous, impossible, absurd.
PETER. But at the moment, you can't think of anything else to do.
HELEN. Apart from sending for the police, which I always might.
PETER. What are you going to wear? You can't be Farthingale in that.
HELEN. I refuse to wear anything else.
PETER. There's a black dress in your cupboard.
HELEN. That's years old. (*Change of tone*.) You've been looking through my clothes!
PETER. Well, of course. Black dress, shoes; I suppose the stockings will have to do. Hurry up. She'll be here in a moment.
HELEN (*going towards the bedroom door*). You do understand—
PETER. Yes, I do understand.
HELEN. Well, as long as you understand—
PETER. Which I do, please hurry.

           (*She goes out.* PETER *goes up to the chest which is used as a sideboard and takes out a pair of table napkins. He puts them on the table and goes over to the kitchen. At the kitchen door he turns*.)

   Farthingale!
HELEN (*off*). What?
PETER. Have you an apron?
HELEN (*off*). What?

SCENE I] OUT OF THE CROCODILE 19

PETER. An ordinary white apron without "Hullo and Good-bye" printed on it in twenty-five languages.
HELEN (*off*). On the shelf beside the fridge.
             (PETER *goes off. After a moment he calls out.*)
PETER (*off*). No, no!
HELEN (*off*). What?
PETER (*re-entering*). "His." No good at all. (*He goes across to the sideboard and takes from the drawer a small lace cloth.*) I've found just the thing in the sideboard.
HELEN (*off*). That's for a tea-table.
PETER (*throwing it through the half-open door*). Try it.
HELEN (*off*). It's a bit sort of—
PETER. Well, I dare say you were a bit sort of when you were younger. Pin it on.
HELEN (*off*). Wait a moment, I've just remembered.
PETER (*vaguely*). Good. (*He stands looking round.*) Readjustment, that's the problem. I'm generally a bachelor living on my own, doing myself quite well, of course, but pigging it in a quiet way. You know how things get when a man is on his own; a little bit dusty, a little bit drab, enough to excite pity. (*He blows at the mantelpiece.*) Though not so bad as to inspire action. But Farthingale keeps the place spick. (*He picks up* HELEN's *knitting and drops it into a vase.*) Unless she's getting beyond it, of course; that might be so. Poor old F! That's what I call you; F doesn't see as well as she used to. Can't whisk about with the feather duster like she did in the old days.
             (HELEN *enters wearing the lace cloth as an apron and on her head an elaborate maid's cap.* PETER *looks at her for a moment in astounded silence.*)
That's overdoing it.
HELEN. Not when we have company.
PETER. Where did you find it?
HELEN. There was a suitcase full of things that belonged to my Aunt Edith.
PETER. She was a maid?
HELEN. Of course not; she had a maid, called Freeman, though I don't know what's wrong with being in service.
PETER. Nothing, F, nothing; it looks very smart.
HELEN. I prefer to be called Farthingale in company.
PETER. Oh, very well.
             (*Door bell. They both look towards it.*)
Here we go.
             (*After a moment's hesitation* HELEN *goes out towards the front door.* PETER *stands in front of the fireplace.* MONICA's *voice is heard.*)
MONICA (*off*). Is this Mr. Hampster's flat?

HELEN (*off*). Yes, miss, what name shall I say?
MONICA (*off*). Parsons.
                    (HELEN *enters, followed by* MONICA.)
HELEN. Miss Parsons.
PETER (*coming towards her*). Monica, how very charming you look. Farthingale, take Miss Parsons' coat.
HELEN. I was going to. (*She helps* MONICA *off with her coat, which she takes into the bedroom.*)
MONICA. Who's she?
PETER. That's old Farthingale, bless her; something of a Tartar, but a heart of gold, pure gold. Cigarette? (*He offers her the box and she takes one.*)
MONICA. Do you mean she's yours?
PETER. Actually, I think of myself as hers.
                    (HELEN *re-enters as* MONICA *sits.*)
A light for Miss Parsons, please, Farthingale.
                    (HELEN *takes a table lighter from the sideboard and lights* MONICA'S *cigarette.*)
Lunch in five minutes.
HELEN. It's not nearly ready yet.
                    (PETER *coughs warningly.*)
Master Peter. (*She goes out.*)
PETER. She regards herself as one of the family.
MONICA. I never imagined you'd have a maid; you said you lived all on your own.
                    (PETER *goes across to the cupboard.*)
PETER. So I do; after all, one has to keep one's distance. I mean she wouldn't like it if I was always hanging about the servants' quarters. Sherry?
MONICA. Thank you. Does she sleep here?
PETER. She doesn't sleep at all—at least, I've never caught her at it. Tell me about yourself.
MONICA. Me?
PETER. I know so little about you.
MONICA. There's nothing to know.
PETER. Oh, but there is, about everyone.
MONICA. I live at home and I go to work.
PETER. Work, ah yes; do you like your work?
MONICA. Not specially, but it's work; one's got to do something.
PETER. You must see a lot of unhappiness.
MONICA. Why?
PETER. Homes broken up, bailiffs put in, families cast into the street, all for the lack of a few shillings.
MONICA. I don't see anything like that; I work in the office.

SCENE I]   OUT OF THE CROCODILE   21

PETER. But the letters you must have to write, "Dear Sir, We would call your attention to Clause 2 of your agreement—"
MONICA. They're not my letters.
PETER. You write them.
MONICA. I don't read them.
PETER. Never?
MONICA. No, I mean it's not as though they were to people I knew.
PETER. Supposing they were?
MONICA. That would be different.
   (PETER *nods, satisfied that the ground is well prepared.*)
   What do you do?
PETER. Guess.
MONICA. I couldn't.
PETER. You might. Think of a profession for me.
MONICA. You're not a doctor.
PETER. I'm afraid not.
MONICA. A barrister.
PETER (*hesitating for a moment*). No.
MONICA. An architect?
PETER. Ah.
MONICA. You don't look like one.
PETER. I'm not at my drawing-board. When I am I run my fingers through my hair and wear a crumpled smile. I look all right.
MONICA. Where is your drawing-board?
PETER. You shall see it next week.
                      (HELEN *re-enters.*)
HELEN. Luncheon is served.
PETER. Good.
   (*He indicates a chair for* MONICA *and sits opposite her.*)
   I hope you're hungry.
MONICA (*sitting*). What sort of things do you design?
PETER. Houses, you know, and flats and hospitals, churches, schools. Anything they ask for. Cathedrals if wanted.
MONICA. Aren't you young to do cathedrals?
PETER. Not small ones.
   (HELEN *has gone into the kitchen and now returns with two plates of smoked salmon which she serves first to* MONICA *then to* PETER.)
   Ah, smoked salmon, what a surprise. You know what I like, don't you, Farthingale? (*To* MONICA.) She spoils me.
   (*The door bell rings. For a moment* PETER *is shaken. He looks at* HELEN. *She is uncertain what to do.*)
   Oh no! Not now! I don't care if it's an order for a monastery, it will have to wait. Tell them to go away.
   (HELEN *goes towards the door.* PETER *talks fast to* MONICA.)

Never a moment's peace does one get. If they're not ringing up they're hammering on the door. Sometimes I think of having the telephone disconnected, but one has an obligation to the public—
(HELEN *has opened the door to reveal* HENRY *standing outside. He starts to come in, then looks at her with astonishment.*)
HENRY. Oh, terribly sorry, wrong flat.
(*He steps back and* HELEN *shuts the door.* MONICA *has seen none of this, her back being to the door.*)
PETER. Was it for me, Farthingale?
HELEN. No, sir, a person mistook the floor.
PETER. What did he think it was, the ceiling? Ha ha.
HELEN. You will have your joke, Master Peter.
(*She moves towards the kitchen.* PETER *addresses* MONICA.)
PETER. Some lemon? As I was saying about an obligation—
(*The door bell rings again.* HELEN *turns round and goes to it.*)
They're very persistent today.
(HELEN *opens the door.* HENRY *is still there.*)
HENRY. It is my flat, it is.
PETER (*to* MONICA). Excuse me—(*He rises. He addresses* HENRY.) Hove!
HENRY. What?
PETER. Hove, back again.
HENRY. I'm Hampster. Who are you?
PETER. Back after all these months.
HENRY (*to* HELEN). Who is he?
PETER (*to* HELEN). Take Hove to the servants' hall and give him some food.
HENRY. I don't understand, Helen. I don't understand what's happening.
(*By this time* HELEN *has bustled him off to the kitchen.* PETER *resumes his seat.*)
PETER. I'm terribly sorry about this. Wouldn't have had it happen for the world.
MONICA. Who is he?
PETER. Hove? Oh—Hove was our first footman.
MONICA. A footman?
PETER. Yes, we ran to a couple, you know, in the old days. I don't know what happened to the other one. But when the old place came under the hammer Hove refused to leave it, very devoted, so they sold him with it, and a good price they got for him, too.
MONICA. You can't sell people as though they were houses.
PETER. No indeed, there's a buyers' market in people; still it was a good price and Hove was proud to have fetched it. But then they turned the place into a girls' school and the only job they had for him was in the boiler-room. Well, it was a come-down, as you can imagine. I

mean a first footman expects to be a butler one day; he doesn't expect to be a boilerman. Something happened to him. Do have some more brown bread.
MONICA. Thank you. What happened?
PETER. Sitting among the boilers he became convinced that he was in the engine-room of a ship. You know, the steady hum, the glowing of the furnaces and the house above him forging through the dark sea.
MONICA. The house?
PETER. To us the house, to Hove an Ocean Greyhound.
MONICA. Oh.
PETER. He might have gone on stoking happily for years, only he began to worry. Where was the captain? Where the crew? What had happened to the chief engineer? In the end he persuaded himself that they had all jumped overboard and the ship was heading for the rocks. He took to rushing up in the middle of the night and sounding the fire alarm, crying "Abandon Ship"!
MONICA. So they sacked him?
PETER. Not exactly; staff were hard to come by; they ignored him. After a time there was a fire and they were all burned in their beds.
MONICA. How terrible.
PETER. Terrible, yes. It was the end of Hampster Hall. And now—(*He waves a hand around.*) Here I am; happier in a way, of course. I mean, one has more of a chance to be oneself. Integrity, I think, is the word I want.
MONICA. But it's sad to think of it all gone.
PETER. Not quite gone. There's me, and there's Farthingale, and sometimes there's Hove, though he's not quite all that he might be these days. You can never be absolutely certain what he'll say.
　　(HENRY *enters, carrying a tray. He puts it on the sideboard, removes* MONICA's *plate and then* PETER's. *All this in complete silence. He seems as though he were going to protest at any moment.* PETER *studies him, weighing him up.*)
A fine day, Hove, is it not?
(HENRY *pauses, carrying the tray, on his way out. He deliberates.*)
HENRY. The outlook is unsettled. I would advise a raincoat for this afternoon—(*Pause.*) Sir.
　　　　　　　　QUICK CURTAIN

　　　　　　　　SCENE 2
A few hours later.
　　The remains of an elaborate tea can be seen; cake-stand, silver kettle, and so on. It is still daylight and the blinds are raised. PETER *is*

at the door of the flat saying good-bye to another girl who is as different from MONICA as possible.
PETER. It's been lovely seeing you and I'll let you know as soon as possible. Good-bye, Laura.
(*He comes back into the room holding a manuscript which he throws on the sofa. He takes a piece of bread and butter from a plate and eats it.* HELEN *and* HENRY *enter from the kitchen.*)
That's your gas bill for another quarter. (*He finishes the bread and butter and takes out his diary.*) You cut it too thick.
HENRY. Look here, it won't do.
PETER. Oh, it'll do, but it's too thick if we're going to have the silver out.
HENRY. That was my great-aunt's kettle.
PETER. So I told her.
HELEN. No, you didn't; you said it was yours.
PETER. Yours, mine, ours.
HELEN. Nothing of ours is yours.
(PETER *drifts over to the telephone, still looking at his diary.*)
PETER. You may clear the tea-things.
HELEN. We will not.
HENRY. We've served two meals and that's enough.
HELEN. Two meals in our own flat to complete strangers.
PETER. Have a cake. (*He offers her a plate of cakes.*)
HELEN. No, thank you.
(PETER *offers it to* HENRY, *who hesitates, wanting a cake, but not sure which to take.*)
PETER. One normally takes the nearest.
HELEN. We don't need to be told how to behave.
(HENRY *has taken the nearest cake and is eating it.*)
PETER. I think you do. (*He points to* HENRY.) He served twice from the right at lunch and you made no attempt to warm the teapot.
(HENRY *tries to say something, but his mouth is full of cake.*)
What?
HELEN. He said we are not your servants.
HENRY (*swallowing*). That's right.
PETER. We've had this out already. What else can you possibly be?
HENRY. You could be our servant.
PETER. Oh no, not at the moment. There's far too much to be done this week-end. (*He lifts the telephone and dials.*) If I can find the time I'd like to take the rating officer on the river tomorrow, but it depends on your bank manager. (*He speaks into the telephone.*) Eileen? What? Oh, sorry, could I speak to her, please? What! (*Hand over telephone, he speaks to the others.*) Oh, my God, she's gone to Birmingham.

HELEN. For good?
PETER. Not for our good. (*Into telephone.*) You don't happen to know who's taken her place at the bank? Ah, oh—have you? (*He makes a sign to the* HAMPSTERS—"*It's this girl.*") Well, my name's Henry Hampster.
HENRY. Me, me, me!
(PETER *and* HELEN *both hush him.*)
PETER. Known as Peter. Ah, she did, did she? Well then, I wonder if you'd have pity on me—pity I said. No, I didn't mean pity, not really. I mean would you come out to the cinema with me? Yes—I mean no—(*He makes a face at the receiver as if to say "What sort of girl is this?"*) Oh, good. Well, as we don't know each other by sight, we can't very well meet at the cinema, and as Eileen was going to call round here, perhaps you'd do the same and have a little something first. A little something—no, nothing in particular, just anything. Well, something is anything, in a way. (*To the others.*) Isn't it? You know the address? Good. In about ten minutes then. I'm looking forward to it. 'Bye. (*He puts down the receiver.*) Am I hell looking forward to it! That's a very literal-minded girl.
HELEN. Why has the other girl gone to Birmingham?
PETER. Oh, I don't know. Why do girls go to Birmingham? I suppose they send them there. This one's taken over her flat as well as her job. Eileen was easy; she was romantic. This one—(*He shakes his head.*) I don't know. "Julia Fawcett." Tells you nothing. I shall have work to do. (*He picks up a manuscript from the sofa.*) And the gas board has written a novel. It's about a girl who works in an office. (*To* HELEN.) You wouldn't care to read it?
HELEN. No.
PETER. Then I must. She wants an opinion. Each to his task. (*He moves towards the bedroom.*)
HELEN. Where are you going?
PETER. To lie down. I can't read this standing up. Put some glasses ready. (*He goes out.*)
HENRY. Now, will you please explain?
HELEN. I have explained, twice.
HENRY. But I didn't understand. How could I understand when you kept sending me in here with food?
(HELEN *starts to clear the tea-things.*)
HELEN. You must serve and take away from the left, never the right.
HENRY. I know that, but I don't understand.
HELEN. You will when you're bankrupt, and that's what we'll both be if you aren't careful. (*She takes a tray out to the kitchen.*)
HENRY. Is he going to stay here all the time? (*He receives no answer and*

goes across to the bedroom door. He looks through the keyhole. HELEN *re-enters.*)

HELEN. Henry!
HENRY. He's lying on the bed.
HELEN. You mustn't look through keyholes.
HENRY. It's my keyhole, my bed, my door, my flat.
HELEN. Then why haven't you paid your rent? That's what I don't understand.
HENRY. No, no, I'm the one that doesn't understand—me, me!
HELEN. How could you let things slide? You must have known you weren't paying it, and the gas, and the light, and the bank.
HENRY. I never open bills.
HELEN. Utterly impossible.
HENRY. You told me not to; you said it made me bad-tempered.
HELEN. Oh, nonsense.
HENRY. You most certainly did!

(*The bedroom door opens and* PETER *looks in.*)

PETER. A little less noise, please.

(*He retires. They drop their voices.*)

HELEN. There—
HENRY. It was at breakfast-time, the year the Oval was flooded.
HELEN. Whenever it was it doesn't matter now. Here we are in this mess and we can't get out of it.
HENRY. We can go down to Brighton.
HELEN. I couldn't leave the flat knowing that he's here; besides, there's a lot to be done.
HENRY. What?
HELEN. Tea to wash up, supper to get.
HENRY. Cold in front of the television.
HELEN. But he's got this girl coming. They'll want something after the cinema.
HENRY. Look here, you're not—not—not his servant.
PETER (*calling, off*). Hove!

(HENRY *stands for a moment, uncertain what to do.* PETER *calls again.*)

Hove!

(HELEN *makes a sign meaning* "You'd better go to him." HENRY *goes.* HELEN *picks up the tea-tray and is going towards the kitchen as* HENRY *comes out of the bedroom.*)

HENRY. Ashtray, he wants an ashtray. (*He takes one off the sideboard.*)
HELEN. Not that one; it's dirty.

(*She goes out.* HENRY *picks up a silver one, looks at it, breathes on*

it, *rubs it on his elbow and takes it into the bedroom as* HELEN *reappears to plump up cushions and generally straighten the room.* HENRY *comes in from the bedroom and goes to his drinks cupboard.*)
HENRY. He wants the sherry in a decanter.
HELEN. You'd better wash it out.
HENRY. Of course. (*He starts with the decanter towards the kitchen. Half-way there he stops and shouts at the bedroom door.*) I'm not your servant!
(HELEN *takes the decanter from him.*)
HELEN. The bottom's terribly stained.
(HENRY *puts the neck of the decanter to his eye and squints down it.*) Lead shot is what you need; you put some in water and shake it round.
HENRY. I haven't got any shot; I'll just have to wash it and hope for the best.
(*He goes into the kitchen.* HELEN, *still clearing the tea-things, sees some crumbs on the floor. With a guilty look towards the bedroom door she quickly brushes them under the hearth-rug with her hand.* HENRY *re-enters.*)
Look here, I've just thought.
(HELEN *picks up the tray.*)
Is he going to be here all night?
HELEN. I suppose so.
HENRY. Difficult.
HELEN. We'll talk about it later. I've got my work to do.
(*She takes the tray out.* HENRY *goes up to the table on which the cigarette-box stands. He takes a cigarette, then with a guilty look at the bedroom door he shovels four or five into his pocket. He puts one in his mouth and is about to light it when* PETER *enters from the bedroom, holding the manuscript.* PETER *looks at him.* HENRY *defiantly lights his cigarette and blows out a large puff of smoke.* PETER *raises his eyebrows slightly and flops into a chair. He indicates the manuscript.*)
PETER. This is dreadful. If she goes on writing novels, you'll have to pay your gas bill.
HENRY. Look here.
PETER. Yes?
HENRY. This can't go on.
PETER. Why not?
HENRY. There isn't room in the flat.
PETER. I can't help that; you know where you're supposed to be.
HENRY. But it's mine, all mine.
PETER. And Farthingale's.
HENRY. She's mine, too, and she's not Farthingale—she's my wife.
PETER. What's she doing now?

HENRY. Washing up tea and getting supper.
PETER. I didn't ask for supper.
HENRY. She thought you might want to bring your—bring the bank manager back here after the cinema.
PETER. Mm, I don't know; it might help. Candles, let's have some candles. I don't know what sort of girl she is, but they might easily help. One has to play these things off the cuff.
HENRY. I should think you're good at doing that.
PETER. I've had practice.
HENRY. How did you sort of latch on to us?
PETER. I was sitting on the front at Brighton one week-end. Just left my job and I was turning over various possibilities in my mind; prison, suicide, work, when you came past with your wife.
HENRY. Sunday morning.
PETER. Yes.
HENRY. We take a constitutional on Sunday morning.
PETER. From the West Pier to the Clock Tower.
HENRY. And back.
PETER. That's right. You strolled along enjoying the sea air and I was struck by your look of—what shall I call it?
HENRY. Health?
PETER. Not exactly.
HENRY. Not wealth.
PETER. No, though you didn't look poor. It's hard to describe; contentment? No, not quite that. I know what it was; you looked impeccable.
HENRY (*pleased*). Oh, did we?
PETER. You looked as though you had absolute control over your surroundings, as though you decided the height of the tide and the velocity of the wind.
HENRY. One doesn't quite do that, you know.
PETER. But you looked as though you did. "Mr. and Mrs. Impeccable" I called you to myself and I followed you. I hoped that if I got near you some of the impeccability would rub off on me.
HENRY. You made damn sure it did.
PETER (*holding up a hand to check him*). No, no, wait. You were nearly home when a crack appeared in the whole fabric of my fantasy. Your wife got a bit of grit in her eye.
HENRY. No harm in that, an accident.
PETER. Accidents don't happen to the sort of people I thought you were. It meant that you weren't impeccable, just ineffable. Your wife took her handkerchief out of her pocket and her keys fell to the ground. I picked them up, and later on I used them.
HENRY. Those keys! Oh, those keys! (*He goes quickly to the kitchen*

door.) Helen, we've found the keys we lost the day you got something in your eye. Do you remember?
(HELEN *comes to the door*.)
HELEN. The ones I dropped getting out of the car?
HENRY. Oh, no, no! Or yes; you said you must have dropped them getting out of the car, I said you'd lost them on the front when you took out your handkerchief.
HELEN. Well?
HENRY. You did lose them on the front when you took out your handkerchief.
HELEN. No, it was when I got out of the car, I'm sure.
HENRY. But it wasn't; it was on the front. (*Pointing to* PETER.) He was there; he picked them up.
HELEN. You can't be sure they were the same keys.
(*She goes out.* HENRY *drums with his fists on the back of an armchair. He suddenly realizes that* PETER *is watching him with interest. He gathers himself, moves to the fireplace, then with his back to it speaks ferociously to* PETER.)
HENRY. Anyway, you shouldn't have kept them!
PETER. But I admired you so much, I wanted to see where you lived and to be like you.
HENRY (*pleased*). Oh, did you?
PETER. Yes, I wanted to be ineffable, too. I wanted to know how you did it.
HENRY. I suppose it's mainly a matter of breeding. You know, one does things because one does them and not other things because one doesn't.
PETER. It was a dreadful disappointment to find that once your front door closed you were about as effable as anyone could be. (*Shakes his head*.) Sad.
HENRY. We have never claimed to be anything that we aren't.
PETER. Oh yes, you have; you've claimed to exist and you don't.
HENRY. If I hit you on the nose you'll know I exist.
PETER. Not really, only that my nose does.
HENRY. I've a jolly good mind to.
PETER. If my nose bled I couldn't take your bank manager to the cinema.
HENRY (*shouting*). My bank manager is my bank manager and your nose is nothing to do with him!
PETER. Her.
HENRY. Him, him. I know him. I've met him!
PETER. When?
HENRY. Mind your own business.
PETER. How many years ago?

HENRY. It doesn't matter; he's still there.
PETER. You had a bank statement the other day.
HENRY. I may have done.
PETER. What did it say?
HENRY. That's my business.
PETER. You don't know.
HENRY (*airily*). I've a fair idea.
PETER. You don't know, because you never opened it.
HENRY. A man has a pretty good notion of his financial standing without actually having to look at the figures.

(PETER *goes to the desk and opens the bottom drawer. In it is a mass of unopened envelopes so closely packed in that they spring out as the drawer opens.*)

Leave my things alone. (*He nervously looks towards the kitchen.*) Put them away quick.

(PETER *is selecting an envelope.*)

PETER. Here we are.

(HENRY *goes across to him and starts packing the other envelopes back in the drawer.*)

HENRY. I don't like bothering Helen with financial details. (*He slams the drawer shut and turns back to* PETER, *who is holding the envelope.*) Give me that.

(PETER *slits it open and hands him the statement.* HENRY *looks at it, bemused.* PETER *turns it the other way up.*)

PETER. Look at the balance.

(HENRY *does. He is silent. He walks to the fireplace, then turns and speaks in a strangled voice.*)

HENRY. Nine million pounds, fifteen and threepence.

(PETER *nods.*)

I'm nine millionaires. (*He goes to the kitchen door.*) Helen!
HELEN (*off*). I'm busy.
HENRY. Helen, I'm rich—we're rich, look!

(HELEN *comes on.*)

HELEN. What?

(HENRY *waves the statement at her.*)

HENRY. Nine million pounds in black.
PETER. It could just as easily be in red.

(HENRY *turns towards him.*)

HENRY. But it isn't in red, it's in black.
HELEN (*looking at it*). It's a misprint.
HENRY. How do you know?
HELEN. Obviously.
HENRY. I see nothing obvious about it; I mean here it is down in black —and white.

HELEN. You don't imagine you've made nine million pounds without noticing.
HENRY. Do you think you're more likely to be right than the bank?
HELEN. They can make mistakes.
HENRY. We all make mistakes; I do and you do.
HELEN. And the bank.
HENRY. But on balance, that's all I say, on balance which—now be honest—which is most likely to make a mistake, you, Helen Hampster, or the London and Home Counties Bank? Think of it, just for a moment, think. Have you got two hundred million in reserve? Have you an Earl for a director? Have you got branches all through Kent and Sussex and Surrey, and Paris—yes, a branch in Paris—have you?
HELEN. I've got enough common sense to know a mistake when I see one. (*To* PETER.) That's what it is, isn't it?
PETER. Of course.
HENRY. Leave him out of it.
HELEN. You can't. I expect his girl friend made the mistake.
PETER. Not exactly. The machine made the mistake; all Eileen did was to fail to cross it out.
HELEN. There!
HENRY (*dejected*). Well, in that case how much money have I got?
PETER. At a rough estimate—and mind you it can only be a rough estimate—I should say none.
HELEN. He's got his salary. (*She snatches the statement from* HENRY *and starts leafing through it.*) That's paid in every month. (*She begins to look puzzled. There is a silence. She reaches the last sheet.*) It isn't there. (*To* HENRY.) Where is it? Where is your salary? You told me it was paid into the bank.
HENRY. It was.
HELEN. Where is it now?
HENRY. I think a man called Ashworth gets it.
HELEN. He takes your salary? Why?
HENRY. Because they gave him my job when I left. He'd been after it for years.
HELEN. When did you leave your job? Why did you leave your job and why didn't you tell me?
HENRY. I can't really remember when; some time ago.
HELEN. Then why?
HENRY. You told me to.
HELEN. I what?
HENRY. You said, "They don't appreciate you; if I were you I'd go somewhere else."
HELEN. When did I say that?

HENRY. Two years ago, when I was telling you why we couldn't have a new car. "They don't appreciate you; if I was you I'd go somewhere else."
HELEN. Where did you go?
HENRY. Sometimes to the public library, sometimes for a walk, sometimes to the park.
HELEN. Do you mean to tell me that for the last two years, when I thought you were working, you were reading and walking and sitting?
HENRY. That's what I did when I was working.
HELEN. Deception! Utter deception!

(*The door bell rings.*)

PETER. And that will be your new bank manager.
HENRY. What do we do?
PETER. Keep out of the way.
HENRY. Where?
HELEN. Bedroom. (*She dashes towards it.*)
PETER. No, she might want to use the bathroom.
HENRY. Kitchen.
PETER. And like mice.

(*They go off into the kitchen.* PETER *shuts the door. He then goes up to the door of the flat and opens it.* JULIA *stands there.*)

JULIA. Are you—er—?
PETER. Yes, I am, if you're Julia. Do come in.

(JULIA *makes no move.*)

JULIA. We were going to the cinema.
PETER. It's not quite time. Come in.

(*Encouragingly he tries to wave her into the room, but still she stands in the doorway.*)

JULIA. Well—
PETER. Please—
JULIA (*cautiously stepping forward*). Is there a bed?
PETER (*pointing to the bedroom*). In there, yes, not in here.

(*She enters further as* PETER *shuts the door.*)

JULIA. I'm not prudish; don't think I'm prudish, will you? But it's one of the things I'm not supposed to do. At least, not till I'm twenty-one. You see, Daddy promised me a thousand pounds if I didn't smoke or drink or anything at all really until my twenty-first birthday. It's very sensible; instead of just having to say "no", I can say "no, because", and people understand.
PETER. I do—yes, I do—I quite understand. Do sit down.

(JULIA *sits.*)

Cigarette?

(*She looks at him reproachfully.*)

Oh, sorry.
  (*He puts down the cigarette-box and sits.* There is a moment's
  pause.)
  You are allowed to go to the cinema?
JULIA. Oh yes, and to the theatre, and night clubs, and anywhere I like.
  Mummy and Daddy trust me absolutely. They think that's best.
  For instance, I've always been allowed to read anything I wanted.
PETER (*with interest*). Oh yes? And what do you read?
JULIA. Mostly about animals, but I don't have to. I could have read all
  those silly books they go on about, and Mummy and Daddy wouldn't
  have said a single word. So naturally, I don't bother.
PETER. What sort of animals?
JULIA. Horses mostly. I love horses, but dogs, too, and really any
  animals at all. Actually one of my favourites is about a family of
  mice.
PETER (*bleakly*). We might go to the zoo one day.
JULIA. Oh no, I think animals ought to be free, not penned up in cages.
PETER. Like you in the bank?
JULIA. I don't see that.
PETER. Behind bars.
JULIA. Well, actually I work mostly in an office at the back.
PETER. On a machine?
JULIA. Yes.
PETER. Like—(*He tries to remember.*)
JULIA. Like Eileen, yes, but even so one can't complain about the bars;
  they're there to keep people out.
PETER. So you like it?
JULIA. Not as much as I'd have liked a stables, but it's all right.
PETER. You don't find it frustrating to see all that money on one side of
  the counter, and all those people without it on the other?
JULIA. Oh no, that's life, and the hours are good.
        (*Voices are heard from the kitchen.*)
  Who's that?
PETER. Nobody, nobody, mice.
JULIA. They're saying words.
PETER. Talking mice.
      (*She looks at him sharply. He has gone too far; he has to make it a
  recognizable joke.*)
  In little hats and coats. No, it's probably people next door—thin
  walls. (*He stands.*) Time we went.
JULIA. I thought we were going to have something.
PETER. We've had a little talk. I can't think of anything else that won't
  cost you a thousand pounds.
        (*She rises as he goes up to open the door.*)

O.C.–C

JULIA. There's food.
PETER. Oh, food later. You wouldn't want to miss the cartoon. It's about two rabbits.
JULIA (*about to go out*). Your hat.
PETER. Hat?
JULIA. Don't forget your hat.
PETER. I need a hat?
JULIA. Of course you do; you're going out.
                    (PETER *wanders vaguely* D.S.)
PETER. Hat? Hat? Hat?
         (*The kitchen door opens a fraction and a bowler hat is handed out to him as he goes past.*)
         Hat!
JULIA. Why, that was just like magic.
         (PETER *puts the hat on and looks at himself in a mirror.*)
PETER. Dreadful!
JULIA. It fits you very well.
PETER. That's what's so dreadful. I don't understand it.
         (*He is at the door, he takes off his hat, ushers her out and they go.* HENRY *and* HELEN *come out of the kitchen.*)
HENRY. What a nerve. Shocking nerve. Why should he go to the cinema in my hat?
                    (HELEN *is tidying the cushions.*)
HELEN. He hasn't got one of his own.
HENRY. That's absolutely no reason at all. (*He flops down on the sofa.*)
HELEN. No, not there; I've just tidied it.
                    (HENRY *half rises, then sinks back.*)
HENRY. Damn it, I don't care; this is our flat, not his.
HELEN. Nothing's ours now, thanks to you.
HENRY. Blame me, I knew you would. I always am, just for trying to keep things running.
HELEN. Running? You? When you leave your job and pay no bills and hide all your letters like a squirrel. Don't imagine I don't know what's in that drawer. (*She points to it.*)
HENRY. You know?
HELEN. Of course, I looked.
HENRY. Why didn't you say anything?
HELEN. Because you'd have resented it and made a stupid fuss.
HENRY. You didn't want to know about them.
HELEN. I did know about them.
HENRY. But you didn't want to face the facts; you pretended there was nothing in there.
HELEN. Well, what did you do?
HENRY. I've my own ways of doing business.

HELEN. Yes, look at them, look at us; we don't exist any more, all because of your weakness and refusal to face facts.
(On the last line she pulls the drawer so hard that it comes completely out and the letters cascade about them. HENRY *stands looking at them helplessly.)*
Come on, we'll get down to them now. *(She kneels and picks out a letter which she hands to him.)* You open that.
(She opens one herself. HENRY *slowly opens his.)*
A gas bill in red; it says we're going to be cut off.
HENRY. When?
HELEN. A year ago last December. What's that?
HENRY. A thing about how to get five pounds a week from the age of fifty-five.
HELEN. There, you see, you've thrown away an opportunity.
HENRY. It would mean paying five pounds a week until I was fifty-five.
HELEN *(holding another letter)*. I wrote this one.
HENRY. No!
HELEN. To you from hospital.
HENRY. You haven't been to hospital for ten years.
*(*HELEN *does not answer; she is engrossed in her own letter.)*
Then it was only for two days, I expect the reason I hadn't opened it was because you arrived back before it did.
(Still no answer. HELEN *turns the page.* HENRY *picks out another letter and starts to read it.)*
A regimental dinner. I couldn't have gone of course—Saturday night—we'd have been in Brighton. *(He shakes his head.)* Chubby Claymore, poor old Chubby, I wonder what's happened to him.
HELEN *(folding up her letter)*. Love.
HENRY *(still reading)*. "A good turn out."
HELEN. I sent you my love.
HENRY. I should have gone, you know; in a way I feel I've let poor old Chubby down.
HELEN. Kisses, too.
HENRY. They were a grand lot of chaps. *(Sadly he puts the letter down and picks up another one.)*
HELEN. You might at least have opened it.
HENRY. I say, here's a letter from His Majesty's Secretary of State for War; it's thanking me for helping them.
HELEN. What?
*(*HENRY *hands it over to her.)*
HENRY. "During the recent grave Emergency."
HELEN. It only says they don't need you any more.
HENRY *(snatching the letter back)*. It says what I said it says, thank you,

and that I can go on using my rank. (*He thinks for a moment and then speaks again.*) "Captain Hampster"; you know I might have been anything if I'd stayed in.
HELEN (*sarcastic*). Anything.
HENRY. It's easy to mock.
HELEN. Oh, come on, let's get through them. (*She opens several letters very quickly, then stops at one.*) You to me.
HENRY. No.
HELEN. "Helen my darling, my beloved, my angel."
HENRY (*looking over her shoulder*). That's not my writing.
HELEN. Whose is it, then?
HENRY. Some other fellow. I say, this won't do.
HELEN. But it's signed Henry.
   (HENRY *takes it and scrutinizes it.*)
HENRY. Not by me. (*An idea strikes him and he ferrets around among the open letters until he finds the one he wants.*) Here we are—look, that's your writing; it's from you to you.
HELEN. Nonsense.
HENRY. You can see perfectly well that it is.
HELEN. Why should I write letters to myself and call myself Henry?
HENRY. I haven't the faintest idea.
   (HELEN *studies both letters for a moment, then lets them drop as though they were of no importance. She picks up another.*)
HELEN. How many times have I told you to renew your driving licence?
HENRY (*vaguely*). Goodness knows. Here's one of my school reports. (*He smiles.*) It says I'm promising, and good at algebra, but I need to take more care with my written work.
HELEN. You haven't any written work.
HENRY. I had then. (*He reads the bottom of the report.*) And I was a good influence in the House.
HELEN (*who is reading another letter*). Well, I hope you don't think you are now.
HENRY. I know what I am now.
HELEN (*abstractedly reading a letter*). Good.
HENRY. Who's that from?
HELEN. It's to me.
HENRY. But from?
HELEN. Nobody you know.
HENRY. Yourself again?
HELEN. No, from Veronica Carraway.
HENRY. Who's she?
HELEN. I said it would mean nothing to you.
HENRY. Tell me who she was and then it will.

SCENE II] OUT OF THE CROCODILE 37

HELEN. A girl I knew at school. (*She smiles.*) I must have been captain of netball when she wrote this.
(HENRY *holds out his hand.*)
No, it's personal.
HENRY. It must be thirty years old.
HELEN. Twenty-five. All right, at least it shows I was appreciated once. (*She hands it to him.* HENRY *looks at it.*)
HENRY. Good Lord—I say—Why did she put your hair ribbon under her pillow?
(HELEN *shrugs.*)
HELEN. Not everybody's as lacking in affection as you are.
HENRY (*who is looking at another letter*). You didn't have a hair ribbon when I met you. (*He reads for a moment.*) I don't call this lacking in affection. It must have been my first term at prep school. (*He hands it to* HELEN.)
HELEN. To your mother, how did that get in here?
HENRY. I suppose with some of the stuff we cleared out when she died. (*He rises and paces up and down remembering.*) I was beaten for sending that letter, with a slipper.
HELEN. But there's nothing awful in it.
HENRY. No, but all our letters were read by the headmaster to make sure we didn't say rude things about him or the food. The trouble was, you see, that I called her Mop.
HELEN. Yes, why?
HENRY. Oh, I don't know—a joke; but if you wrote anything odd like that he'd read it out in front of the school and they'd all laugh at you. So on the second Sunday I wrote a secret one and on the afternoon walk I dropped out of the crocodile.
HELEN. You what?
HENRY. Dropped out of the crocodile.
HELEN. Oh yes, of course, that crocodile.
HENRY. I pretended my shoelace had come undone beside a letter-box, and popped the letter in, but Mr. Randall—he took French and Games—saw me do it and reported me. (*He shakes his head sadly.*)
HELEN (*looking at the letter*). Did she come and take you away?
HENRY. No.
HELEN. Did you cry when they beat you?
HENRY. Only a little, when I was alone.
(HELEN *digs amongst the letters once more. She takes out a large envelope.*)
What's that?
(HELEN *opens the envelope. She takes out two documents which she looks at.*)
HELEN. Both our birth certificates.

HENRY. Give me mine. (*He snatches one from her.*)
HELEN. Don't snatch.
HENRY. I've a right to my own birth certificate.
HELEN. That's mine you've got.
HENRY. Well, give me mine.
HELEN. Here you are. I don't want it.

    (*They change them over.* HENRY *rises and moves over towards the fireplace, reading.* HELEN *reads hers sitting on the floor.* HENRY *nods slowly to himself, as though confirming that every word was true.*)

HENRY. It's all there.
HELEN. I never discovered what my parents were doing in St. Albans.

    (*Both of them seem to have been struck by a kind of silent melancholy.* HENRY *looks from the documents to the pile of letters.*)

HENRY. Let's burn this lot and start again.
HELEN. Start?
HENRY. From here. (*He taps his birth certificate.*) After all, look at us. Well, I mean—just look, something must have gone wrong.
HELEN. But how will burning all this help?
HENRY. It's as though it were all on my shoulders, as though I couldn't stand up straight.
HELEN. I know what you mean.
HENRY. Then we'll burn the lot and see what happens. (*He starts to gather up a pile of letters.*)
HELEN. Burn them unopened?
HENRY. Yes, yes, they've answered themselves; they're in the past.
HELEN. Of course, we can't really burn them.
HENRY. Why not?
HELEN. We can't burn anything in this flat; there's no fire.
HENRY. And that's wrong; there should be. (*He looks at the letters in his hand.*) The dustbin, I suppose.
HELEN. No, they might blow about. There's our new machine.
HENRY. Of course, of course, the Eliminator! (*He heads for the kitchen with an armful of letters and pauses at the kitchen door.*) Will it eat paper?
HELEN. It eats small bones.
HENRY. And cardboard—yes, it'll manage paper.

    (*He goes off.* HELEN *starts to gather up letters. From the kitchen comes the high whine of the machine.* HENRY *bustles back in.*)

It likes them.
HELEN (*handing him a pile of letters*). Don't overfeed it.
HENRY. It won't mind, it's greedy.

    (*He goes off.* HELEN *gathers up more letters.*)

HELEN. The man did warn us.

    (*She goes off as* HENRY *comes on.*)

HENRY (*gathering up another armful*). That was oyster shells and tins.

(HELEN *comes on.*)
HELEN. And wood—paper's made of wood.
HENRY. Not always, sometimes it's made of rags.
(*He goes off.* HELEN *picks up another load.*)
HELEN. Only the very best paper.
HENRY (*off*). Besides, it's pulped.
HELEN. What?
HENRY (*re-entering*). Pulped, mashed up. (*He shows with his hands just how it is pulped.*)
HELEN. What do you think the machine's doing?
HENRY. That's quite different. (*He takes a load of letters from* HELEN *and carries them off.*)
HELEN. I don't see why. I mean if you mash up wood to make paper, and then you mash up the paper, surely you're half-way back to wood.
HENRY (*off*). It doesn't work like that.
(HELEN *is replacing the drawer.*)
HELEN. How do you know?
HENRY (*re-entering for another pile*). I know.
HELEN. You say you do.
HENRY. Because I know, I know. (*He goes off with the last of the letters.*)
HELEN. Anybody'd think you'd invented the machine the way you're so cocksure about it.
(*She shuts the drawer, picks up an odd letter lying on the floor, looks at it, tears it up and puts it in the wastepaper basket. The machine is turned off and* HENRY *re-enters.*)
HENRY. There, that's done. I feel better already. (*He goes to* HELEN *and takes her hands.*) Don't you?
HELEN. I feel odd.
HENRY. Oh, Helen. (*He clasps her round the waist.*)
HELEN. Very odd.
HENRY. We're still quite young, you know.
HELEN. Well, yes.
HENRY. I mean we can start again.
HELEN. I thought we had.
HENRY. Not yet; we're sort of waiting for the start. Like before a race.
HELEN. Perhaps that's what seems odd.
(HENRY *wanders round the room.*)
HENRY. Quite different I shall be; I don't smoke, I don't drink. I think I shall become a farmer; that's what I always wanted to be. We'll sell our lease and the Brighton flat and buy a farm. Cows, pigs, sheep, live in the open air, wonderful.
HELEN. What about me?

HENRY. Farmer's wife. Big kitchen. (*He points to the ceiling.*) Bacon up there, hens, eggs and lots of—
HELEN. Children?
HENRY. Well, yes, yes—Yes, yes, I suppose—
HELEN. It's too late.
HENRY. Oh, I don't know.
HELEN. Much too late.
  (HENRY *pauses, considering. After a moment he sighs, deflated.*)
HENRY. Of course, you're perfectly right. (*He picks up his birth certificate.*) We don't really need these.
HELEN. I believe they're helpful.
HENRY. To whom?
HELEN. To the person who registers your death.
HENRY. Oh. (*He picks up his own and* HELEN's *and replaces them in the drawer.*) Well, they'll be in there.
HELEN (*pointing to the clock*). Half past six.
  (HENRY *cheers up.*)
HENRY. So it is, time for a noggin. A drop of What Killed Auntie.
HELEN. I'll see if there's anything on.
  (*She goes over to the television set and switches it on.* HENRY *goes to a built-in cupboard by the window from which he produces a bottle of gin and a bottle of whisky.*)
HENRY. A quiet evening at home—just the job.
  (*As he moves the sofa to face the* T.V. *the sound comes on. Dance music is being played.*
  From now on all their movements have the assurance and rhythm of a ritual dance and whatever they are doing they keep half an eye on the screen.
  HENRY *draws the curtains and they set about making themselves comfortable for the evening.* HELEN *places a small table at one end of the sofa,* HENRY *does the same at the other.* HENRY *puts a bottle of gin on the* D.S. *table and a bottle of whisky on the* U.S. *one.*
  HELEN *has gone out to the kitchen. She returns with a tray containing a loaf of sliced bread, a hunk of cheese, some butter and a bunch of bananas, together with plates, knives, etc. These she puts on a low table in front of the sofa.*
  HENRY *puts his tobacco jar at his end and checks that he has matches, pipe, etc. Both of them sit.* HELEN *pours herself a tumbler of neat gin.* HENRY *does the same with the whisky.*
  They are about to drink when HENRY *puts down his tumbler and leaps up. He rushes round the room collecting all the ashtrays that he can find and placing them in a semicircle round the sofa. He sits again. He raises his glass, half to* HELEN *and half to the* T.V. *screen and drains the tumbler.* HELEN *does the same.* HENRY *sighs.*)
I needed that.

SCENE II] OUT OF THE CROCODILE 41

HELEN. It's nice to relax.
(*The music comes to an end. A* WOMAN ANNOUNCER *is heard.*)
ANNOUNCER. For the third of our programmes on Forensic Medicine, "The Body of the Court", we are taking you to Paddington Green mortuary, where Sir Jocelyn Figg is waiting to perform a post-mortem.
(*Background music follows as the titles come up.* HELEN *and* HENRY *have started to eat, drink and smoke more or less at the same time, their eyes never moving from the screen. Sometimes they become a little muddled,* HENRY *finds that he has filled his pipe with cheese,* HELEN *that she has three cigarettes alight simultaneously and, in fact, appears to be smoking a banana. The* PATHOLOGIST *begins to speak.*)
PATHOLOGIST. Good evening. We are in luck tonight, because only an hour or two ago the body of a young woman was recovered from the Regent's Canal, and thanks to some person or persons unknown we are able to show you another facet of our work. Here's the little lady—As you can probably guess, she has been in the water for some considerable time—(*His voice starts to speed up around this point until it is unintelligible cackling.*) First we remove the stomach, which will be sent with its contents to our Cricklewood laboratories for analysis, and now we force the rib cage open so that we can take a look at the lungs, which will tell us whether or not death is due to drowning—
(*The light begins to fade outside. By the end of this sequence the* HAMPSTERS *are only lit by the flickering from the screen. We hear a great roar of audience laughter, merging into snatches of music, odd lines of dialogue, shots, the roar of engines, the squeal of tyres, and any other sound effects that will serve to indicate that an evening's television is passing.*
Suddenly the door opens and PETER *and* JULIA *enter. We are now back with a recognizable programme.*)
ANNOUNCER. "Did you or did you not administer poison to your wife?" There is a pause. He does not know what to say.
(PETER *has switched on the light.*)
PETER. My parents.

CURTAIN

ACT TWO

Scene i

Positions are as at the end of Act One. The voice from the set speaks again.

ANNOUNCER. Did you dismember her and dispose of her remains through the post?
  (JULIA *steps forward with a social smile as* HENRY *stands.*)
JULIA. How do you do?
  (HENRY *blinks bemusedly.*)
PETER. Hullo, Father. I brought Julia back.
JULIA. Don't let me disturb you, please.
  (HENRY *turns off the set.*)
HENRY. That's all right, we weren't watching. Lot of rot anyway.
  (*He shakes hands effusively with* JULIA.)
How d'you do? How are you?
  (*He calls out to* HELEN, *who is still sitting looking at the screen.*)
Helen—
HELEN (*vaguely*). They never said good night. (*She comes to.*) Oh—
PETER. Mother, this is Julia.
  (HELEN *stands unsteadily.*)
HELEN. Mother?
PETER (*sulkily*). Mummy. (*To* JULIA.) They never want us to grow up, do they?
  (HELEN *pulls herself together; although slightly fuddled, she is in full control of the situation. She shakes hands with* JULIA.)
HELEN. Julia, is it? Do sit down—Peter dear, don't just stand there; bring up chairs, move the sofa, be useful.
  (PETER *starts to move the sofa back to its original position. He nearly knocks over the bottle of whisky, which is rescued by* HENRY.)
HENRY. Steady now, watch what you're doing.
HELEN. Boys are so clumsy, aren't they?
JULIA. Do you live here, too?
HENRY. Oh yes.
PETER. They use it as their home when they're in London, don't you?
  (HENRY *considers this statement and to his pleasure finds it to be the truth.*)
HENRY. Yes, we do, as a matter of fact.
HELEN. We have a flat in Brighton.
HENRY. But we use this as our home when we're in London.

SCENE I]   OUT OF THE CROCODILE   43

JULIA. I love Brighton.
          (*She and* HELEN *are now sitting.*)
HELEN. You must come and see us there. Peter can take you on the Pier. I expect you'd enjoy that.
HENRY (*flourishing the bottle*). Care for a drink?
PETER. She doesn't.
HELEN. Let her answer, darling. Manners. (*To* JULIA.) Would you?
JULIA. No, thank you, really.
HELEN. Tea. Let's all have tea. Peter, you know what to do.
PETER. Me make tea?
HENRY. Yes, why not? Can't expect your mother to do everything.
HELEN. Take some cups and saucers from the cupboard and put them on a tray—the round one would be best—then the little green milk jug with some milk in it, and a bowl of sugar.
HENRY. With some sugar in it.
HELEN. And you're not to eat more than one lump.
PETER (*in a fierce whisper*). You're making me much too young.
HENRY. Don't talk to your mother like that.
HELEN. There's plenty of time to grow up. Then you put a little boiling water in the pot to warm it and empty it out into the sink.
PETER. Where's the water?
HELEN. In the kettle. You put the kettle on and light the gas. (*She gets up.*) Oh no, perhaps I'd better do it; you might burn yourself.
PETER. I can do it. Of course I can. I'm not a baby. (*He has gone out into the kitchen.*)
HELEN. It seems only yesterday that he didn't exist at all.
          (HENRY *motions again with the bottle to* JULIA.)
HENRY. Are you sure you won't?
JULIA. Quite sure, thank you.
HENRY. I think I will. (*He pours himself an enormous whisky.*) We use this as our home when we're in London.
HELEN (*to* JULIA). We have a flat in Brighton.
JULIA. Yes.
          (PETER *returns, standing in the doorway.*)
PETER (*sulkily*). Where are the spoons?
HELEN. In the silver drawer, darling, where they always are.
PETER. I've looked there.
HELEN. You can't have looked properly.
PETER. I have looked properly. I've looked twice, and there aren't any teaspoons there at all.
HELEN. Then they're in the bowl.
PETER. No, they aren't.
HELEN (*rising*). Oh dear, oh dear, one always has to do things in the end.
JULIA. Don't for me, please. (*She rises.*) I really ought to be going.

PETER. Yes, I'll see you home.
HELEN. Oh no, darling, it's too late. Henry, you see her home.
HENRY. Yes, oh yes, by all means, yes.
JULIA. There's no need. It really isn't far.
HELEN. But at this time of night—
PETER. I took Julia out and I shall see her home.
HELEN. You'd have to come back by yourself and it's much too late.
PETER. Oh, for heaven's sake!
HELEN (*to* JULIA). I think someone's overexcited and it's time he went to bed.
HENRY. That's right. Run along, old chap.
PETER. I will not.
HELEN. Don't be defiant.
JULIA (*edging towards the door*). I shall be perfectly all right.
                    (PETER *moves up to her*.)
PETER. Come on, I'll see you home.
HENRY. You will do no such thing. Go to bed at once. You insolent young puppy, how dare you defy your mother!
PETER (*to* JULIA). I'm sorry about this. I really am.
HELEN. Do as your father says, dear.
PETER. He isn't my father.
HELEN (*outraged*). Peter!
PETER. And she's not my mother. I'm sorry, but it was all a silly sort of joke. I'll explain on the way home.
JULIA (*stiffly*). No, please don't come. I'd rather go alone.
PETER. But you must let me explain.
JULIA. You have. It was some kind of joke and I expect it was very funny, and I must go now.
HELEN. Aren't we your parents any longer?
PETER. No, never again.
HENRY. But we do use this as our home when we're in London.
          (HELEN *sits dabbing her eyes with her handkerchief.*)
What a pity. It was really rather nice. (*To* JULIA.) Do stay and have some tea. Or anything.
JULIA. Is this really your flat?
HENRY. Yes, we use it as—
PETER (*breaking in*). All right, she knows what you use it as.
JULIA (*to* PETER). I don't believe you've told me a word of truth all evening. I'm sorry, but I can't stand people who aren't absolutely frank with me.
HENRY. You're quite right, my dear. I couldn't agree with you more. One must be frank with people.
HELEN (*to* PETER). You see where not being frank has got you.
PETER. Me? My God, me?

SCENE I] OUT OF THE CROCODILE 45

HELEN (*to* JULIA). I really do apologize. It was an abominable way to treat you.
JULIA. No, no, it was my fault. I shouldn't have come in the first place. It was stupid of me to go out with someone I'd never met.
    (*She is not far from tears.* HELEN *goes up to her.*)
HELEN. You mustn't let it worry you. It might have happened to anyone.
HENRY. Come to think of it, it happened to us.
PETER. What did?
HENRY. You did.
JULIA. What?
HELEN. He happened to us just as he happened to you. He simply uses us all.
    (*A great revelation suddenly descends on* HENRY.)
HENRY. Oh, my word! Oh, my goodness!
HELEN. What is the matter?
HENRY. I've just remembered, him, her, everything.
PETER. And about time, too.
HELEN. Oh—yes, sandwiches. (*To* JULIA.) You mustn't go; there are sandwiches.
HENRY. And candles, and music, and wine! (*He wanders around, still vague but excited.*)
JULIA. No, not for me.
HELEN. Yes, yes. All for you. (*She goes out into the kitchen and hands a candle out to* HENRY.)
PETER. I'd laid on a little party; they'd forgotten.
JULIA. It's too late now.
HENRY. Never, never, never too late.
    (HELEN *enters with a plate of sandwiches.*)
HELEN. Here you are, sandwiches; it's not every day we entertain a bank manager.
PETER. No, no, she's not.
HENRY. You said she was.
PETER. In a jocular way, as though you were a corporal and I called you a general.
HENRY (*with some indignation*). I was a captain.
HELEN (*to* JULIA). These have fish paste in them, and these have something else. Do take one, please. I made them specially for you.
    (JULIA *takes one.*)
JULIA. Thank you.
HENRY. But she is our bank manager.
PETER. Oh, will you keep quiet!
HENRY. No, I won't. You said she was and here she is.
JULIA. Is your account with us?

HENRY. Yes.
PETER. Such as it is—ha, ha, such as it is.
HENRY. It's nine million pounds in black.
HELEN. Henry, it's very vulgar to talk about money.
HENRY. Not to a bank manager. (*He struts up and down a bit.*) Nine millionaires, that's me, nine big cigars, nine private planes, eighteen diamond cuff links—and yet we live very, very simply. Have another sandwich.
  (*He indicates the plate which* HELEN *thrusts forward at* JULIA, *who takes one.*)
HELEN. We owe you such a lot.
PETER. Yes, well I expect Julia would like to go home now, wouldn't you, Julia?
JULIA (*coldly*). I'm eating a sandwich.
HELEN. Don't hurry her.
  (*She takes* JULIA *by the arm and leads her to a chair.*)
Sit down again, my dear, and tell us how you manage.
JULIA. I don't really because— I mean I'm not actually the manager. That's Mr. Folder.
HENRY. Of course it is. I knew the name, but it went right out of my head—now it's back again. Folder, that's it, "Yours sincerely, T. W. Folder, Manager."
PETER. Tie a knot in yourself, and remember it then. Folder's your man; he's the chap who knows all about your affairs.
HENRY. But he doesn't—oh no, not the half of them. (*Pointing to* JULIA.) She's the one who manages my bit of the bank.
HELEN. And manages it very well.
JULIA. I only work a machine.
PETER. A marvellous machine. Buzz buzz, and it adds, ting-a-ling, it subtracts, much faster than you or I could do it, and far better.
JULIA. Oh yes, it's cleverer than me, even though maths were my strong point at school.
HENRY. Were they, were they really? That's very interesting. They were my weak one—would you believe it? They were. Shows how little they really matter, I suppose.
JULIA. Oh, but they do!
HENRY. To you perhaps—yes, yes, I can see that; though of course all you really have to do is not to draw a line.
  (PETER *goes up to him and speaks in a very low voice with great intensity.*)
PETER. This—this is it!
HENRY. What?
PETER. This is where you draw one.

HENRY. I'm talking about the line she doesn't draw when the machine makes a mistake and gives me nine million pounds.
(*There is a long pause.*)
HELEN. Henry, I don't think you should have said that.
JULIA. I must go. Please don't bother to see me home; it's perfectly all right.
(PETER *moves to stand between her and the door.*)
PETER. Meaning that it isn't.
(JULIA *looks from one to the other. Then puts the question boldly.*)
JULIA. What have you been doing? Tell me at once, or I'll call the police.
HELEN. My dear child, there's no need for that.
JULIA. I think so. I think you've been doing something wrong and dishonest. I think you've been cheating the bank.
HELEN (*with a silvery laugh*). Oh, really—!
JULIA. Then what have you been doing?
HENRY. Nothing, absolutely nothing. (*But he is beginning to feel ashamed.*)
PETER (*quietly to* JULIA). That's true.
JULIA. I think you're lying.
HELEN. Charming.
JULIA. What else am I to think?
HENRY. I'll tell you the truth. I will—(*To the others.*) No, don't interrupt me. I want to tell the truth. I must. (*He points at* PETER.) He's been living here when we were at Brighton and at Brighton when we were here—for years. And he's been taking out all the girls who look after us—girls like you, I mean—and making up to them so that they don't send us all the letters and bills and things that they write. And when your machine made a mistake and credited me with all that money—
HELEN. It's a joint account.
HENRY. Us, then, he persuaded—(*He snaps his fingers.*)
PETER. Eileen.
HENRY. Yes, Eileen, not to do anything about it.
JULIA. And you went to the bank and cashed cheques?
HENRY. Well, no, mostly I use the pub on the corner.
JULIA. But you've had money that didn't belong to you.
HELEN. Not knowingly. You must realize that. He had no idea.
HENRY. Well—
HELEN. Of course you had no idea.
HENRY. Things did seem a bit easier. Sometimes I wondered why.
PETER. And you were afraid they'd stop being easier if you asked questions.

HELEN. We don't need any clever remarks from you. It's entirely your fault.
(JULIA *picks up the telephone*.)
What are you doing?
JULIA. It's not for me to decide who's right and who's wrong. It's quite obvious there's been dishonesty somewhere and I must report it.
HENRY. She must, you know; she's quite right, perfectly right. I'm with her all the way.
(PETER *shrugs disgustedly and walks across the stage, hands in pockets, morose.*)
PETER. If there were hangwomen you'd commit murder.
HENRY. We'll all feel better when it's cleared up.
PETER. What do you think is going to happen? Six of the best and a handshake from the Headmaster? Not a bit of it. Questions first, men in mackintoshes, the Fraud Squad.
(*He turns to* HELEN *in a hectoring manner.*)
Who paid the household bills, you or your husband?
HELEN. Neither of us.
PETER. Someone did once.
HELEN. Oh, yes.
PETER. Well?
HELEN. Me.
PETER. And then you stopped. Why?
HELEN. There weren't any.
PETER. That suit you're wearing. How did you pay for that?
HELEN. By cheque.
PETER. What did it cost?
HELEN. I can't remember.
PETER. Let's see the cheque-book.
HELEN. I don't know where it is.
PETER. Have you destroyed it?
HELEN. I don't know.
(*She is nearly in tears.* HENRY *steps forward.*)
HENRY. Stop bullying her.
PETER. That's what it will be like. (*To* JULIA.) Won't it?
JULIA (*who still holds the telephone*). I'm sorry, but I have to do it.
PETER. Then about three years each. Wormwood Scrubs for you and me—(*He indicates* HELEN.) Holloway for her.
HELEN (*to* JULIA). You can't do it to us!
JULIA. I must.
PETER. For her own sake. After all, if she didn't she'd be one of us.
HELEN. I don't know what makes you think of yourself as one of us. We haven't told any of these terrible lies.
(JULIA *is about to dial.*)

PETER (*brightly*). Lies? Lies! Yes, lies!
(JULIA *looks at him*.)
You can't believe a word I say.
JULIA. If you're trying to slide out of it, it won't do.
PETER. Certainly not, though, of course, you are going to look very foolish if you bring a lot of policemen round now, and then it turns out that there was nothing in it. (*He becomes a bank manager*.) "Really, Miss Fawcett, the most charitable explanation is that you lost your head. I need hardly point out the infinite harm that you have done to the bank's good name by such an unwarranted slander on one of our most respected customers."
HELEN. It's a joint account.
PETER. "You seem to have taken the word of this unreliable young man and, there's no other word for it, panicked."
(JULIA *replaces the telephone, indignant*.)
JULIA. I never panic.
PETER. Good.
JULIA. I keep calm! I always keep calm! I'm well known for keeping calm!
HELEN. How splendid.
JULIA. But you needn't think you're going to get away with it. (*She moves towards the door*.) I shall find out first thing in the morning.
(HENRY *takes a step towards her, so does* HELEN, *hopefully proffering the plate of sandwiches*.)
If you try to stop me I'll shout for help.
PETER. Let her go.
HENRY (*to* JULIA). But what do you expect us to do?
JULIA. As far as I am concerned you can just jolly well stew in your own juice. You've asked for it.
(*She goes*. HENRY *and* HELEN *look at* PETER.)
HELEN. Now what?
PETER. A certain amount of thinking.
(*They think*. HENRY *takes off his jacket*.)
HENRY. It's late, it's much too late.
HELEN. But we must think of something. Now; we must. First thing in the morning they'll be here.
PETER. No, they won't; it's Sunday. She won't do anything till she's been to the bank, and she can't do that till Monday.
HENRY. That's all right, then.
HELEN (*to* PETER). Did you know that all the time?
PETER. Yes, of course.
HENRY (*going up towards his bottle of whisky*). I say, how jolly good. How splendid, we've got an extra day, and Sunday, too. (*He pours himself a drink*.) Saturday night.

PETER. There's hardly any time at all.
HENRY. Oh, don't be so gloomy.
HELEN. I'd like a drink, too.
HENRY (*looking round*). Gin, gin, gin—I drink whisky, she drinks gin. (*To* PETER.) That's marriage.
        (*He finds the gin and pours* HELEN *a large one*.)
What'll you have?
PETER. It's no use settling down to a party; we've got to think.
        (HENRY *hands* HELEN *her glass; she curls up in the chair. He makes himself comfortable on the sofa*.)
HENRY. No need to flap, old boy; plenty of time for thinking in the morning.
HELEN (*yawning*). The best thing to do is to sleep on it.
HENRY (*putting his feet up on the sofa*). Nothing like sleeping on things.
        (PETER *looks towards the bedroom door and looks at the* HAMPSTERS.)
PETER. No, I suppose there isn't.
HENRY. My father always used to say, if you've got a problem sleep on it, and when you wake up it will probably turn out not to be a problem at all.
HELEN. When you see things in daylight they look quite different.
        (PETER *has gone quietly into the bedroom and shut the door behind him. The* HAMPSTERS *are busy ruminating over their drinks*.)
HENRY. I would like to have all my clothes taken off.
        (HELEN *glances at him a little startled*.)
All my clothes taken off and my pyjamas put on, and be in bed without moving.
HELEN. There should be an invention.
        (HENRY *drains his glass*.)
HENRY. Sometimes I don't really like whisky at all.
HELEN (*indistinctly*). Drink gin.
HENRY. It makes me cry.
        (HELEN *drinks and puts down the glass. Her eyes are shut*.)
HELEN. Whisky doesn't make me cry. (*She kicks off her shoes*.)
HENRY. It makes you angry. Last time you drank whisky you hit me.
(*He kicks off his shoes*.)
HELEN. With a saucepan. (*She laughs slightly to herself*.)
HENRY. A saucepan.
        (*A pause*.)
Stew in our own juice. (*With distaste*.) In our own juice.
HELEN (*very sleepily*). Horrid.
HENRY. Hell!
HELEN. What?
HENRY. I've left the light on at the door.
HELEN. I'll turn it out.

HENRY. You won't, I know you won't; you'll go to sleep with it on. I'll have to do it. I will; yes, I will.
  (*He heaves himself off the sofa and pads to the door, where he turns out the light without really having opened his eyes. He pads back again to the sofa and collapses on it. There is a pause.*)
  Helen—Helen—
HELEN. Hmm?
HENRY. If dishonesty's wrong, how shall we live? How shall we live, Helen? How?
  There is a delicate snore from HELEN *in reply. The lights go down to a complete* BLACKOUT.

SCENE 2

It is morning. Sunlight filters through the blinds. Church bells are ringing outside.
  HENRY *is asleep on the sofa.* HELEN *is curled up in a chair.* HENRY *twitches. Slowly he wakes.*
HENRY. Sunday.
  (*He gets up and shuffles off into the kitchen, yawning. After a moment he comes out again. He goes towards the sofa, but half-way there something strikes him as odd. He turns back and has a look through the kitchen door. He looks round the room without taking it in, then sees* HELEN. *He shakes her lightly.*)
HELEN (*sleepily*). Mm? Oh. Mm?
HENRY. Helen.
HELEN. Is it late?
HENRY. I don't know, but, Helen, something odd.
HELEN. What?
HENRY. I went to the bathroom and it wasn't a bathroom—it was a kitchen.
HELEN. You were dreaming. (*She settles down to sleep again.*)
HENRY. I don't think so.
  (*He walks round the room, taps one or two bits of furniture, then raises the blind, flooding the room with light.* HELEN *groans.*)
HELEN. Oh no!
HENRY. I knew there was something wrong!
HELEN. It's too early for Sunday.
HENRY. We're not at Brighton.
  (HELEN *sits up and looks round.*)
HELEN. No.

HENRY. And we're not in our bedroom. (*With triumph.*) That's why the bathroom was in the kitchen. I wasn't dreaming.
HELEN. You said the other way round.
HENRY. Don't care, don't care. (*With sudden horror.*) Oh God! Oh dear!
HELEN. Whisky isn't good for you and you always wish you hadn't. I don't know why you do.
HENRY. Don't you remember? (*He points to the bathroom door.*) Him!
HELEN. Oh yes! And her.
HENRY. And us and everything.
HELEN. Where's she?
HENRY. And Sunday morning.
HELEN (*pointing to the bedroom*). Is she in there? With him?
HENRY. I don't know.
HELEN. Well, you should know. It's your flat.
HENRY. That's what I kept saying yesterday, but nobody took any notice.
HELEN. Find out. Knock on the door.
HENRY. This isn't the usual sort of thing I do on a Sunday. (*He tries the door handle.*) Locked!
HELEN. Tell them to come out.
HENRY (*quiet*). Come out.
HELEN. Louder.
HENRY. Come out!
    (HELEN *gets up, goes across to the door and bangs it.*)
HELEN. Come out of there at once. Come along. At once. We know you're in there.
    (*The door opens and* PETER *appears wearing a dressing-gown over shirt and trousers.*)
PETER. What on earth do you think you're doing?
HELEN. Where is she?
PETER (*to* HENRY). Good morning.
HENRY. Oh, good morning.
HELEN. Where is that girl?
PETER. Julia? I don't know. Not in here.
    (*He indicates the bedroom.* HELEN *looks in.*)
HELEN. The bathroom.
PETER. Go and look.
    (HELEN *goes off.*)
HENRY. The bathroom's in the—No, it isn't, not now. I don't know where I am and it's Sunday morning. You've spoilt my Sunday morning.
PETER. Monday morning's your worry.
HENRY (*pointing*). That's my dressing-gown.

PETER. Tomorrow morning.
HENRY. That's my dressing-gown.
PETER. Every second brings it nearer.
HENRY. That is my dressing-gown.
   (PETER *takes it off and throws it at* HENRY, *who puts it on.*)
PETER. You're for the high jump. Yes, you are. All because of your disgusting habits.
HENRY. I have no habits.
PETER. Food, drink, cigarettes, television. There I was handling a very delicate situation and you don't even try to help. You just go on as you always go on. Like a couple of hypnotized hens with their beaks on a chalk line.
   (HELEN *re-enters in time to hear this last speech.*)
HELEN. And what about you? There you've been without a care in the world, living away at our expense.
HENRY. And now you're trying to spoil our Sunday morning. (*To* HELEN.) I don't see why he should, even though we're not where we ought to be.
PETER. Does nothing sink in?
HELEN. Breakfast. I'll make some breakfast.
   (*She goes towards kitchen.* HENRY *feels his chin.*)
HENRY. Shave—
PETER. Don't you believe it's going to happen to you?
   (HELEN *has reached the kitchen door.* HENRY *is at the bathroom door. They turn towards him.*)
Tomorrow morning is Monday morning.
HENRY. Making this Sunday morning. (*He starts to turn back.*)
PETER. No, wait. At nine o'clock or a little before Julia will go to the bank and she'll see the bank manager.
HENRY. You kept saying she was the bank manager.
PETER. Only according to the Pounce Theory, which is now no more than a picturesque ruin. From now on your bank manager's a real bank manager, your collector of taxes is a true tax collector and your policemen will be one hundred per cent genuine blue-bottles.
HELEN. We don't need policemen.
PETER. The criminal classes never do.
HENRY. Who's a criminal?
PETER. You are. (*To* HELEN.) And you.
HELEN. What nonsense.
HENRY. We've done nothing. Absolutely nothing.
PETER. That is what they will send you to prison for.
HELEN. We weren't to know that all the time we were leading perfectly normal lives you were making us dishonest.

PETER. Turn on me, that's right, turn on me. I knew you would. I give two years of happiness free from financial care and what do I get. Gratitude? No. Peevishness.
HENRY. But we weren't happy.
PETER. What were you, then?
HENRY. Ordinary.
HELEN. Rather dull.
HENRY. And now we're going to be sent to prison for it. (*He sits down heavily.*) It isn't fair.
PETER. You only had to take one good look at yourselves to see how things were going, but you didn't want to.
HELEN. Oh, do stop preaching.
HENRY. Ruining our Sunday morning.
   (*There is a thump on the door of the flat.* HELEN *and* HENRY *turn towards it startled; and there is a pause.*)
PETER. Only the Sunday papers.
HELEN. For a moment—
HENRY. They wouldn't come on a Sunday.
HELEN (*in a sudden panic*). But they will come, Henry, you know they will, and then what shall we do? What shall we do?
HENRY. You know, I could manage a boiled egg.
HELEN. Doesn't it matter to you that you've helped to ruin your wife?
HENRY. Yes, it does, but I could still manage a boiled egg.
HELEN (*turns to* PETER). And you?
PETER. No, thank you. Just toast and coffee for me.
   (HELEN *goes out into the kitchen.* HENRY *makes a half move towards the door.*)
HENRY. Er—? No, I don't suppose it matters. A boiled egg will do.
PETER. What were you thinking of?
HENRY. Fried egg, bacon, sausage, tomato, fried bread, a hearty breakfast.
   (PETER *has wandered over to the window.*)
PETER. Do you find everything looks different? The sky bluer, the trees greener.
HENRY. I believe it's terrible at first, particularly if you're used to something better.
PETER. We've got about twenty-four hours. Rather less perhaps.
   (HENRY *has been looking longingly towards the door of the flat. Now he moves towards it, muttering as though almost ashamed.*)
HENRY. As the papers are there, one might as well have a look at them.
   (*He goes out for a moment and returns with a bundle of papers, reading the headline of the one on the outside. He separates it from the others and throws them on the sofa.*)

PETER *still looks out of the window as* HENRY *sits absorbed in the paper.*)
PETER. Even if the worst doesn't happen, what a life!
(*No answer from* HENRY.)
Everything will be quite different.
(*No reply from* HENRY. HELEN *enters with coffee-cups, etc., on a tray.*)
HELEN. We don't take Sunday papers here.
PETER. I do.
(HELEN *is laying the table.*)
HELEN. At our expense?
PETER. Nothing's at your expense, but it will be soon. (*He raises his voice towards* HENRY.) Tomorrow!
(HENRY *doesn't react.*)
HELEN. There's never a word till he's absorbed the cartoon.
(*She returns to the kitchen.* PETER *picks up a paper and looks at the headlines.*)
PETER. We'll be in next week's.
(HENRY *begins to laugh.*)
I'm glad it appeals to you.
HENRY. Very funny. (*He shows the paper to* PETER.) Very clever.
PETER. Isn't your mind working at all?
HENRY. It has to have some time off. Get stale otherwise.
PETER. We could sell your car. I should think we could do it today; plenty of garages open. I don't know what we'd get, but it would be cash, and that's going to be the problem, actual money in our pockets. Until we get some we can't even begin to plan. (*He wanders round, picking up objects and putting them down again.*) A trip to the East End first. Perhaps Petticoat Lane. We might find a buyer for some of this stuff. You want as little as possible left here when they come; otherwise they'll nab the lot and sell it for next to nothing.
(HELEN *re-enters with two boiled eggs, some toast and a jug of coffee.*)
HELEN. Breakfast.
HENRY. Shave. I ought to shave.
HELEN. Breakfast first.
(*She puts an egg in front of* HENRY *and sits.*)
What's my horoscope?
(HENRY *looks at his paper.*)
HENRY. "Changes are in the air. Good news early in the week removes many of your worries."
HELEN. Good.
PETER. You can't believe that?
HELEN. It's nice to know. Toast?

(*She pours coffee for them as* PETER *sits.*)
PETER. It doesn't mean anything.
HELEN. Still, it cheers one up when it's good. (*To* HENRY.) Eat your egg.
(HENRY *puts aside his paper.*)
HENRY. Mine's dull.
HELEN. What does it say?
HENRY. "Romance solves many problems."
(*He starts on his egg while reading the paper.* HELEN *is doing the same.*)
HELEN. Try one of the others.
(HENRY *picks up another Sunday paper and looks through it. He reads out with disgust.*)
HENRY. "Leo: Affairs of the heart come to a head early in the week and the way seems clear for happiness."
HELEN (*to* PETER). There, you see, they agree.
(HENRY *is now eating his egg, absorbed in the paper.*)
PETER. Simply because the same bit of rubbish appears in two papers doesn't make it true.
HELEN. I don't see you offering us anything more helpful.
(PETER *rises, holding his coffee, and paces restlessly up and down.*)
PETER. I haven't begun to think, but you don't intend to.
HENRY (*looking up*). Intend to what?
HELEN. Think.
HENRY. Oh think. (*He returns to his egg and his paper.*)
PETER. If I had another word with her—(*He moves towards the telephone, then pauses.*) What would I say?
HELEN. You could sort of appeal to her better nature.
PETER. Her worse nature if anything, and I don't think she's got one. Anyhow, it's awkward on the telephone.
HELEN. Ask her round.
PETER. What for?
HELEN. We'll know what she's up to, at any rate. I mean, it won't be just waiting and doing nothing.
(PETER *is about to pick up the telephone, but stops as* HENRY *speaks, indicating the paper.*)
HENRY. There's a man here who chopped up his wife and buried her in a bed of quicklime. At least, he thought he did, but it was ordinary lime and they dug her up perfectly preserved. Think of that.
HELEN. What a stupid mistake.
HENRY. Not a good idea. Anyway, I mean, his own back garden. Far too obvious.
HELEN (*taking toast and marmalade.*) Of course, it's frightfully difficult.

I mean if you've done something like that, well what do you do? If you take the thing somewhere else you're almost certain to be seen and you can't do it on the spot. Even with acid they find out.
HENRY. There could be one way. (*He carefully butters a piece of toast.*) At least, I think there could. I thought of it the moment I saw it. The only possible way in this flat, the way those letters went.
HELEN. If you haven't blocked it up.
PETER. Blocked what?
HELEN. The Eliminator. You know, the thing that grinds up rubbish.
HENRY. I didn't block it up. Paper wouldn't block it up.
HELEN. Anyway, it wouldn't take anything as large as—well, anything large.
HENRY (*seriously and slowly, working it out*). In small pieces it would, quite small pieces, bit by bit, as long as you weren't impatient. (*He turns his egg upside down in his egg-cup.*) Look, I haven't eaten my egg.
PETER. What?
HENRY. Nice fresh egg.
(HELEN *has picked up* HENRY'*s paper and is reading it.*)
HELEN. There'd be traces, you know. They'd be sure to find traces.
HENRY. Oh, I don't know—
HELEN. The head would be the trouble.
(HENRY *absent-mindedly taps the top of his egg, which disintegrates.*)
HENRY. Ha! Fooled myself. Helen, look, I took myself in.
HELEN. You do every Sunday.
PETER. And every week-day, Bank Holidays included.
HELEN. When's your birthday?
PETER. August the fourth.
HELEN. Leo!
HENRY. Like me.
HELEN (*putting down the paper*). Of course! Why didn't you say so before? That's the answer. Here it is in front of us, romance with this girl.
HENRY. Him and her?
HELEN. Then she'll keep quiet.
HENRY (*grumbling*). It's a pretty one-sided sort of horoscope.
HELEN. But a marvellous idea.
PETER. It's a rotten idea.
(HELEN *has started to clear the breakfast-things.*)
HELEN. Why?
PETER (*scornfully*). Romance.
HELEN. Oh, more than that. You must ask her to marry you. (*She goes out.*)
PETER. I don't want to marry her and she doesn't want to marry me.

HENRY. Nobody wants to marry anybody, not when they first think of it, but in the end they do. (*He is feeling his chin.*)
PETER. Why?
HENRY. It's a natural instinct.
PETER. What is?
HENRY. Oh, you know; children, that sort of thing.
PETER. You've no children.
HENRY. No, but—Well, it was different with us. To tell you the truth, when we first got married we kind of took a look at each other and the whole idea seemed so damned improbable that—well, we never did.

(HELEN *re-enters.*)

HELEN. Do go and shave, Henry.
HENRY. I don't know that I need one.
HELEN. Yes, you do, and dress yourself properly. It'll give Peter a chance to telephone.
PETER. I won't, I won't, I won't!
HELEN. Now don't be childish.
PETER. I will not do it.
HELEN. Well, what are you going to do?
PETER. Think. I want to think.
HENRY. We've been thinking. I think all the time. It gets us nowhere.
HELEN. Go and get dressed and don't confuse him.

(HENRY *picks up a paper and goes into the bedroom.* HELEN *clears the breakfast-things during the following scene.*)

She's quite a pretty girl.
PETER. Some of the others are prettier.
HELEN. Looks aren't everything, you know. Not in marriage. It's really rather exciting. How lucky we saw the papers.
PETER. If the stars foretell things, which they don't, they go on doing it whether the papers come out or not.
HELEN. You can't be foretold if nobody tells you.
PETER. No, no. What I'm trying to say is that what happens because of the stars—if anything happens because of the stars—
HELEN. Which you say it doesn't—
PETER. Which I say it doesn't, but if—if—if—then it goes on happening or would go on happening whether anybody worried about it or not.
HELEN. It's all ifs and woulds and whethers with you. Why can't you just read what they say and keep cheerful?
PETER. Because it isn't true.
HELEN. You can make it true.
PETER. But even if I did—I'm not going to, don't think that—but if—
HELEN. Always "if".
PETER. It still wouldn't mean it was true just because it had happened.

HELEN. If you don't think what is happening is true, then you're very hard to please.
(PETER *in an agony of frustration hammers on the back of the same chair that* HENRY *used for this purpose in the previous act.*)
PETER. That wasn't what I meant!
(*The door bell rings.* HELEN *gives a cry.* HENRY *enters from the bedroom, razor in hand. They stand petrified.*)
HENRY. Was it—?
PETER. It was.
(HENRY *goes quickly to the mirror and scrapes away at himself.*)
HELEN. Oh, Henry!
HENRY. One can't go anywhere half shaved.
(HELEN *goes to him.*)
HELEN. They'd give you time to finish. (*To* PETER.) Wouldn't they?
PETER. If it's them.
HENRY. It couldn't be anyone else, not at this hour on a Sunday morning.
(*The bell rings again.*)
HELEN. Perhaps they've mistaken the flat. Perhaps it's a stranger.
(HENRY *dabs at his face with a towel.*)
HENRY. They're all strangers, bound to be strangers. Let them wait.
(*He goes off into the bedroom.* HELEN *watches him go.*)
HELEN. He's always at his best when things are at their worst.
(*Hammering on the door.*)
PETER. They're not quite at their worst.
HELEN. Oh, don't be so gloomy. (*She looks towards the door.*) Will they break it down?
PETER. No. They'll find a master key and open it quite tamely.
HELEN. That gives us a little time.
PETER. What for?
HELEN. Another cup of coffee or even a drink. No, it's too early, but it's a glorious day. (*She starts to let down the blind. It sticks.*) It always does that. I must get Henry to—
(*She breaks off, pauses, and bursts into tears.* HENRY *appears in the bedroom doorway. He wears a blazer and is tying his tie.* HELEN *rushes to him and he puts an arm round her.*)
HENRY. What is it? Helen darling. (*To* PETER.) You've been frightening her.
PETER. She frightened herself.
HELEN. No, not frightened, Henry, only sad. I thought of the blind and asking you to mend it and then I thought, no, it had all come to an end and you never would, and it seemed so dreadfully sad. I'm sorry. (*She sniffs and wipes her eyes.*) Silly. (*She smiles at him.*) Better now.

(*The knocking has died down.*)

HENRY (*giving* HELEN *a comforting pat*). That's the idea. (*To* PETER.) Are they still there?

PETER. Yes. Determined.

HENRY. Well, we can be determined, too. Let's all have a drink.

HELEN. Too early.

HENRY. Nonsense. This is a very exceptional day.

(*He goes to the cupboard and begins to produce glasses and bottles.*)

HELEN. My hair—

HENRY. It looks splendid. Quite beautiful.

(*The door bell has rung again. This time with a continuous peal as though someone had put their finger on the button and kept it there.* HELEN *puts her hands to her ears.*)

Damned impertinence.

PETER. Determined, like I said.

HENRY. You've said altogether too much, that's my frank opinion. I'll give it to you and I've given it to you. Too much by half. You may think you're right—well, perhaps you are right, but I don't care. No, I don't. I don't give a damn for you or anyone else. Or them. No, and I've a good mind to tell them so. Who do they think they are? What do they think I am? Not afraid to face them, I can tell you that. And I'll tell them, by God. Tell them to their faces. See how they like that. (*He has a drink in his hand.*)

HELEN. Henry, Henry! I can't stand it any longer.

HENRY. There, you see. Upsetting my wife. Causing her distress. We'll see about that. (*He moves towards the door of the flat. Half-way across he stops.*) I've got a case against them, you know.

(*He goes into the hall. The other two watch him go. At the last moment* HELEN *makes a slight move as though to call him back.*)

HELEN. Henry—

(HENRY *opens the hall door. There is silence. A moment of blessed relief after the ringing of the bell. Then pause.* HENRY *ushers* JULIA *into the room*).

Oh—

PETER. Good morning.

HENRY. It's keeping fine.

JULIA. I couldn't make anyone hear.

PETER. You did, as a matter of fact.

HELEN. Oh yes.

HENRY. We were delayed.

HELEN. Not ready.

HENRY. Shaving and so on.

HELEN. I'm still not dressed. Isn't it awful? (*She goes towards the bedroom door.*) Neither are you, Henry. Come on.

HENRY. I am.
HELEN. Oh no. You need a clean shirt and those trousers are dreadful. (*She is making little signs to* HENRY *and now speaks to* JULIA.) He'd go about in rags if I let him. All men are like that. Do make yourself at home. We won't be long. Henry!
HENRY. Oh yes, yes, of course. Yes, make yourself at home.
(*He joins* HELEN *and they go out into the bedroom.* PETER *steps towards the bedroom door as though he, too, would escape, but it is shut and he turns back to* JULIA. *Vaguely he indicates the chairs.* JULIA *sits.*)
JULIA. I've been wondering what to do.
PETER. Ah? Oh. Good.
JULIA. I can't believe anything you say.
PETER. It's a fine day, the window's open, the door's shut, you're sitting, I'm standing. (*He sits.*) No, I'm not.
JULIA. Last night—was it true?
PETER. If you can't believe it, perhaps it wasn't.
JULIA. People can't do things like that.
PETER. Perhaps not.
JULIA. But, of course, they do. One reads about them. Swindlers.
PETER. No, no. That's pitching it too strong.
JULIA. What then?
PETER. Ordinary people trying to survive.
JULIA. Ordinary people don't rob banks.
PETER. Really, what an idea. (*He rises and walks up and down.*) As though I went charging about in a mask.
JULIA. It's every bit as bad.
PETER. Nor for the people I don't shoot.
JULIA. But you deceive them and corrupt them.
PETER. Who do I corrupt?
JULIA. There was Eileen, the girl before me. You told her you were a bullfighter.
PETER (*seizing the tablecloth and making a pass with it*). And why not?
JULIA. People aren't.
PETER. Indeed they are. It's a highly respected profession.
JULIA. It's disgusting.
PETER. Why?
JULIA. It's cruel to animals.
PETER. Banks are cruel to people.
(JULIA *leaps up indignantly.*)
JULIA. They are not! They help people all the time.
(*He does a pass with the cloth, dodging her as she advances on him.*)
PETER. Some of the people some of the time.
JULIA. They lend them money.

PETER. So do bullfighters. Here today, gone tomorrow. (*He dodges her again.*)
JULIA. If it wasn't for banks there wouldn't be any money.
PETER. They only breed bulls for bullfighters. At least they don't expect other people to fight them. You bankers, you sit there behind your barricades and watch us struggling with the stuff; twisting, turning, dodging to avoid being gored—(*He suits his actions to his words.*) And when we're down in the blood-soaked sand, what do you do? I'll tell you what you do—you shut away the money and you go home smiling.
JULIA. I don't smile.
PETER. Never at the customers? Surely they teach you to smile.
JULIA. We greet them courteously.
PETER. Courteously, ah! How does one do that courteously? (*Bowing and smirking.*) You're poor, you have no money, get out or we'll run you in. Oh no! Surely not.
JULIA. It's—
PETER. What?
JULIA. It's often—quite often a person's own fault if he's poor.
PETER. Yes?
JULIA. It means he doesn't work or doesn't save. After all, banks want people to have money.
PETER. Bullfighters want bulls to have—Well, to be bulls.
JULIA. Oh, why do you go on and on about bullfighters? I know you're not one and never have been. You aren't the right shape.
PETER. The trousers make the shape. Good God, you're crying. What's the matter?
JULIA (*through tears*). I hate you, the way you twist everything round and try to muddle me and make me think I'm cruel. I'm not and I don't blame poor people for being poor. I don't even like rich people much. All I want to be is honest and sensible, and that's what you ought to be, too.
 (*She looks for a handkerchief.* PETER *hands her the tablecloth. She dabs her eyes with it, then throws it aside.*)
It's no use being nice to me.
PETER. Well, I try being nasty to you and you don't like that. What do you want?
JULIA. Only—only to know for certain.
PETER. Of course, if you were wrong, you'd make an awful fool of yourself.
 (JULIA *doesn't reply.*)
That I call charming. Three people enjoying their last twenty-four hours of normal existence, and you have to come and badger them for your own self-assurance.

JULIA. I hoped it wasn't true.
PETER. Liar. You've been hoping to go to work tomorrow popping with revelation. Think of the excitement. Think of the furious activity. You'll be principal witness, picture in the paper; and they'll talk about it for months.
JULIA. That isn't why I came. I'm not like that.
PETER. Every honest man's like that; and woman.
JULIA. And I suppose by being dishonest, you're not?
PETER. I was. I was. (*He sits.*) I had a job, like you.
JULIA. In a bank?
PETER. No, in a firm. A big firm with an office in the West End and a factory at Slough. I was an executive, a young executive. The policy was youth. Of course, I had an older executive over me. His policy was middle age, but very friendly. Oh, it was a happy office and he saw a future for me in the firm. I had ideas.
JULIA (*sitting*). Yes. I'm sure you had.
PETER. And good ideas, but "Rough at the edges, my dear chap," he used to say. They needed polishing, and of course by the time they were polished they weren't mine any more. They were his.
JULIA. You find people like that everywhere.
PETER. Don't you just! One day I had a real top-grade first-class idea, so I polished it all by myself inside the glass walls of my office until it sparkled, then I went along to—well, call him "X" for executive—and gave him the unpolished version, after which I managed to corner "Z" who was "X's" boss, and told him my idea, sold him my idea, and then described how "X" had blown on it. Well, of course, that did "X" no good, no good at all, and I did it again and went on doing it until the next re-shuffle came and "X" was sacked and I took over.
JULIA. I'd never have expected you to hold down a job like that.
PETER. You think better of me?
JULIA. It shows what you can do if you try.
(PETER *rises and walks away from her.*)
PETER. Yes, doesn't it? When I went into his office to say good-bye to him he was crying. He wished me luck and he was crying: great fat tears soaking into his blotter. (*He turns on her.*) And it was a dreadful firm!
JULIA. He must have been an absolute baby.
PETER. An infant, yes, childish, but what else can you be; faced with—Do you know what we made? One thing only, that's all, a plastic cylinder about that long (*He indicates two inches.*)—with a hole in one side.
JULIA. What for?
PETER. That I never knew. Nobody knew. There was a rumour that it

was part of an electric kettle, but they encouraged it so much that we knew it was a lie.

JULIA. Somebody must have known.

PETER. One of the girls, I believe—yes, one of the top secretaries, she knew what it was for; but, of course, she didn't know what it was— she'd never seen it. And he cried. (*He looks round the room.*) This is a much better way to live.

JULIA. On other people?

PETER. Hampsters aren't other people. You can't call them that. Not them. They're nullities with names.

JULIA (*pointing towards the bedroom door*). But there they are.

PETER. I doubt it. I really do. When they go through a door they're gone, and I should know—I've lived in their absence for years.

JULIA. But it's different now. They're here.

PETER. Nothing is different with them. They don't change. Look at them. (*He flings open the bedroom door and is badly shaken by what he sees. He shuts it quickly, muttering.*) I'm terribly sorry. (*He is very taken aback and moves over to the fireplace.*)

JULIA. What's the matter?

PETER. Nothing, everything. I don't know—(*He reaches down and takes* HELEN's *knitting from the wastepaper basket where he put it the day before. He looks at it.*) Do you knit?

JULIA. Yes.

PETER. And what else?

JULIA. I can cook, play the piano, drive a car.

PETER. Ride a bicycle?

JULIA. Of course.

PETER. Swim, dance, add and subtract, sing, sew, talk French and light a fire with one match?

JULIA. I'm not very good at French.

(PETER *goes to her and takes her hand. He looks at it.*)

PETER. What are you?

JULIA. Good at?

PETER. No, just what?

JULIA. Why do you—have to ask all these questions? Why can't you be ordinary?

(PETER *nods towards the bedroom.*)

PETER. Like them?

JULIA. Like everyone.

(PETER *runs his hand up* JULIA's *arm.*)

PETER. Is this why you came?

JULIA. No.

PETER. Isn't it?

JULIA. No.

PETER. Isn't it?
JULIA. Well—
PETER. Yes?
JULIA. I had to do something. I couldn't sit in my room and look out at backs of houses and wait for the church bells. There was a kind of hope—Oh, why do you make me talk? (*She breaks away from him.*) Everything sounds so silly when it's said.
    (*He stands looking at her, baffled. He perches on the arm of the sofa, still looking at her. She is turned away from him. There is a long pause.*
    He gets off the sofa and picks up the cigarette-box. He half offers it to her and then remembers she doesn't smoke. He goes up to the sideboard, takes hold of a bottle and puts it down again. Slowly JULIA *turns and watches him.*
    He goes to the window and fiddles for a moment with the sunblind. He wanders on and comes to the door of the flat. He steps towards it and stops. For a moment he thinks of going out, then decides not to. He moves down towards the fireplace and runs his hand along the mantelpiece, then blows the dust off his fingers. JULIA *watches him all the time.*
    He stands facing the fireplace deep in thought, then stands on one leg. He takes off his left shoe and examines it. He sits in the chair by the fire.)
PETER. There's a drawing-pin in the sole of my shoe.
JULIA. A knife is the best thing.
    (*She goes into the kitchen.* PETER *tries to take the drawing-pin out with his nail. He hurts it.* JULIA *returns from the kitchen with a table-knife. She kneels beside him and takes the shoe from him.*)
Quite easy with this.
PETER. I hurt my nail.
JULIA. Badly?
PETER. No.
    (JULIA *takes out the drawing-pin.*)
JULIA. There. (*She puts the drawing-pin in the fireplace and starts to undo the laces of the shoe.*) It's terribly bad to take them off with the laces done up.
    (PETER *comes out of the chair, kneels and clasps her to him and kisses her.*)
Oh no—I mean—
PETER. You mean "Yes".
JULIA. Do you?
PETER. Here I am.
JULIA. That's no answer.
    (*He kisses her again.*)
PETER. Is that?
JULIA. I hope it is. I don't usually do this sort of thing at all.

PETER. Nor me.
JULIA. Oh, don't lie, please. I know about you.
PETER. From—(*He snaps his fingers.*)
JULIA. Eileen—
PETER. Yes, Eileen.
JULIA. I'll tell you something.
PETER. Yes, I expect so.
JULIA. I didn't want to go to the cinema with you at all. I thought you'd be just like all the others, that you'd try to hold my hand, and it's so silly because it only gets sweaty and there's no pleasure in it, but you didn't. So then I wondered what you were really like and came back here with you and found out.
PETER. And now I'm different again.
JULIA. Oh, I do hope you are. I couldn't bear it when I liked you and you weren't the sort of person one should like at all.
PETER. Should like?
JULIA. People are either good or bad and the bad ones are horrid.
PETER. So if somebody isn't horrid he can't be bad.
(JULIA *looks at him carefully.*)
JULIA. Are you trying to be clever?
PETER. I suppose that's horrid, too.
JULIA. It's not very nice. A bit showy-off.
PETER. Oh, then I'd better just try to be good.
(JULIA *takes his hand impulsively.*)
JULIA. I hoped you'd say that. I'll do everything I possibly can to help you.
(*She breaks off as the bedroom opens and* HENRY *comes out. He is very spruce in his blazer, regimental tie and well-creased trousers. He stands in the doorway, looking back.*)
HENRY. The weather's holding up well. There'll be quite a crowd today.
(PETER *and* JULIA *watch him in surprise. They are still kneeling and holding hands.*)
(*Calling into the bedroom.*) Don't take all morning. Your face looks fine.
(HELEN *comes out. She, too, is looking her best. She is tying a silk square over her head.*)
HELEN. There'll be a wind on the front.
HENRY. I hope so. I can do with a good blow. Ready?
HELEN. Have you got the key?
HENRY. Of course.
(*By this time they are moving across to the door of the flat and are about to go out when* PETER *speaks.*)
PETER. You are not where you think you are.

SCENE II]   OUT OF THE CROCODILE   67

(HELEN *and* HENRY *look down at them. For a moment they are completely blank. Then they are adjusted.*)
HELEN. I know where I am.
HENRY. Yes, yes, we're here. (*He looks around. He clears his throat.*) Sunday. We take a walk on Sunday.
PETER. I know.
HENRY (*turning towards them, the whole situation descending upon him again*). But now, of course, well—
HELEN. Henry.
HENRY. Yes?
HELEN. Look at these young people.
HENRY. On the floor.
   (PETER *rises and helps* JULIA *to her feet.*)
PETER. It was a question of my shoe.
HELEN (*to* JULIA). Am I right?
JULIA (*with a quick look at* PETER). Well—
HELEN. Yes, I'm sure I am. Oh, my dear, what fun! (*She swoops on her and kisses her, then turns to* PETER.) I think you're a very lucky young man.
HENRY (*pointing*). One shoe off! We can see you've been up to something.
PETER. Us? Us up to something. What about—
   (HENRY *straightens up and fixes him with a stony glare.*)
HELEN. "One shoe off and one shoe on, diddle diddle dumpling my son John."
   (PETER *takes his shoe from* JULIA *and starts to put it on.*)
And we do wish you every possible happiness, don't we, Henry?
HENRY. Yes. Oh yes. Just like us. We ought to have a drink to celebrate.
HELEN. Too early.
HENRY. Oh, I don't know.
HELEN. Much too early. We never drink before twelve on a Sunday. I'll make some more coffee. (*She moves towards the kitchen.*) Come and help me, Julia.
JULIA. May I?
HELEN. You'll need to start finding your way about a kitchen soon.
   (*They both go out.*)
HENRY. Well done! You've done it.
PETER. I haven't done anything. I hardly touched her.
HENRY (*archly*). Ha ha!
PETER. Oh, for God's sake! (*He goes moodily up towards the window.*)
HENRY. Let's have a quiet and quick one. (*He goes to the cupboard.*) Gin? Whisky?
PETER. Brandy.

(HENRY *busies himself pouring.*)
I'm not going to do it.
HENRY. That's what I said to myself the moment I was alone. On top of a bus. But I did it and here I am. Yes, here I am. (*He gives a glass to* PETER.) Astonishing really.
PETER. What?
HENRY. The way one survives. Before you know where you are you'll find you've been married ten years and you'll wonder what happened to them.
PETER. Will I?
HENRY. Yes. Look on the bright side. (*He raises his glass.*) Cheers. (*He hesitates.*) No. (*More firmly.*) No. Not before twelve o'clock. (*He puts his glass down.*) I suppose one should go for a walk, though it wouldn't be the same. It's a mile along the front. One mile and another mile back again. (*He starts to pace around the room, counting his paces, but unwilling to admit that he is doing so.*)
PETER. You're all taking far too much for granted.
    (HENRY *reaches the corner by the kitchen and turns before he replies.*)
HENRY. Oh no. (*He paces up towards the flat door and speaks again.*) Not at all. (*To himself.*) Sixteen.
PETER. I'd rather jump out of the window.
HENRY. Not far enough. You'd land in a flower bed and only break a leg. (*He paces across the back of the stage to* PETER.)
PETER. You've thought of that?
HENRY (*having reached the corner by the cupboard, he stops dead*). Thought? Yes, I've thought of everything. (*He starts again.*) Twenty-five—
PETER. What are you doing?
HENRY. I don't like missing my little walk on a Sunday. It's good for me—sets me up. I was just working it out. Seventy times round this room makes one mile or near enough. They do it on ships, you know. So many times round the deck. (*He starts walking round.*)
PETER. You cut that corner.
HENRY. I did when I counted.
PETER. No, you did not.
    (*He moves towards the door of the flat, which means that he's travelling in the opposite direction to* HENRY, *and demonstrates how* HENRY *should have turned the corner.*)
You went round it like this.
    (HENRY *passes him.*)
HENRY (*cheerily*). Good morning.
    (PETER *comes round past the fireplace in time to meet* HENRY D.S.C.)
One and a half. This won't do. We must go the same way.
PETER. I'm not doing it.

SCENE II]   OUT OF THE CROCODILE   69

HENRY (*walking on*). No compulsion. Volunteers only. Take a seat.
   I'll be back soon. Two. Of course, if you'd like to count, it would be
   a help.
PETER. You're mad.
HENRY. Not a bit of it. One's got to keep fit. Three. One needs some
   easier way of counting. Stone in the pocket, perhaps, like an umpire,
   chuck one out each time—Four—no, too heavy at the start. I know
   what. Yes, I know just the thing—a billiard-marker. Buy a second-
   hand billiard-marker—

   (PETER, *who has become dizzy trying to follow* HENRY, *sits holding
   his eyes.* HELEN *and* JULIA *come out of the kitchen,* HELEN *carrying a
   tray with cups on it,* JULIA *carrying a coffee-pot.* HENRY *strides past
   them beaming and lifting an imaginary hat.*)

   'Morning. Lovely day. (*He continues on his way.*)
HELEN. Stop him.
PETER. I can't.
HELEN. Oh God, he's gone mad!
HENRY. Not a bit of it. Ten.

   (HELEN *thrusts the tray at* JULIA.)

HELEN. You've driven him out of his mind. (*She seizes* HENRY.)
   Henry, stop—do stop. It's all right now. You're not going to prison.

   (HENRY *has stopped.*)

HENRY. Never thought I was.
JULIA. Oh, but—
PETER. What? (*He takes the tray from her.*)
JULIA. Thank you. He might, quite easily.
HELEN. What for?
JULIA. You know.
HELEN. Surely that's all forgotten?
JULIA. Forgotten?
PETER. Forgiven then.
JULIA. Oh, forgiven, yes; but, of course, I can't very well forget, can I?

   (PETER *puts down the tray.*)

HENRY (*jovially*). No, I suppose you'll remember it as one of those
   things that happened when you were young. You'll look back on it
   and think did it really happen? Do you know, once when I was your
   age—
      (HELEN *has sat down at the coffee-tray and has poured a cup of
      coffee. She now interrupts, speaking to* JULIA.)
HELEN. Milk?
PETER. Why should he go to prison?

HELEN. Milk?
JULIA. Thank you. (*To* PETER.) Not only him.
HENRY. Do you mean you're still going to tell people?
HELEN (*pouring milk*). Enough?
JULIA. Fine, thank you. (*To* HENRY.) I must. I mean, if I don't, well, I'd be one of you.
HELEN. I thought that's what you wanted to be.
HENRY. Dammit, you were sitting on the floor holding his shoe.
HELEN. Sugar?
JULIA. Oh, please.
HENRY. You can't send him to prison after that, or me.
PETER. She can.
        (HELEN *hands* JULIA *the coffee.*)
JULIA. Thank you. (*To* PETER.) I knew you'd understand.
PETER. I suppose not robbing banks is included in your thousand pounds?
HENRY. What thousand pounds?
JULIA. It's a sort of bet Mummy and Daddy have made with me.
HELEN (*to* PETER). Coffee?
PETER. No, thank you. She's not allowed to do anything at all until she's twenty-one.
JULIA. And this would be acting a lie.
HELEN (*to* HENRY). Coffee?
HENRY. No, thanks. (*To* JULIA.) How old are you now?
JULIA. Twenty and nine months, and it started when I was sixteen, so it's really hardly worth giving it up now. (*To* HELEN.) You shouldn't have made coffee just for me.
        (HELEN *pours some for herself in silence.* JULIA *is relieved.*)
Oh, good. (*To* PETER.) I'll wait for you.
PETER. I don't believe it. You can't stand there being polite, drinking coffee, talking about Mummy and Daddy and do this to us, all for a thousand pounds.
JULIA. It isn't only the money.
HENRY. No, no, I can see that.
JULIA (*to* HELEN). I'm sorry about the coffee. (*She makes a half move as though she would hand it back to* HELEN.)
HELEN. No, no, that's perfectly all right.
HENRY. Your mind's quite made up?
JULIA. I'm afraid so.
HENRY. Well done—jolly good—I respect you for it.
PETER. Are you trying to talk yourself into prison?
HENRY. Well, no, I don't say that, but one's got to face the music. (*He shakes his head.*) You know, it'll be quite a relief when it happens, in a way; get it off one's chest. (*Reflectively he pats his stomach.*)

SCENE II] OUT OF THE CROCODILE 71

PETER. That's not your chest, and you won't get anything off it. (*He turns back urgently to* JULIA.) Don't you understand? Don't you have a glimmering of what you're proposing to do? Would you do it to a horse, to a dog, to a mouse?
HENRY. Mousetraps.
PETER. Yes, I suppose you would.
JULIA. And so would you, and so would everyone.
HELEN. And quite right, too; it's a silly argument.
                    (PETER *heads towards the door.*)
PETER. All right then, you think of a better one.
HELEN. Where are you going?
PETER. Away.
                    (HENRY *intercepts him.*)
HENRY. Oh no.
JULIA. No, you mustn't go.
    (HENRY *takes him by the arm and leads him away from the door.*)
HENRY. You can't leave us in the lurch.
PETER. I could—oh, easily I could.
HELEN. You won't have the chance.
             (PETER *looks from one to the other.*)
PETER (*in surprise expressing something which he has just realized*). You're Them.
HELEN. Who?
PETER. Them. The great big capital Them, that's why you want to face the music and get it off your chests and all the rest of it, you want Your Policemen to come and take you away. Your Cities, Your Courts, Your Bye-laws and Your Most Obedient Servants. (*He steps towards* JULIA.) Don't you see? Well, don't you, don't you? You can't be so beautiful and not understand.
JULIA. I do understand, but I've explained to you. I've got to do what's right.
HENRY. It's quite insoluble, my dear fellow. Better make the best of it.
                (*Pause.* PETER *ponders.*)
PETER. Not quite insoluble. (*He turns to* HENRY.) Got your cheque-book on you?
HENRY. Yes. (*He produces it.*)
PETER. Write a cheque.
             (HENRY *takes a pen, then hesitates.*)
HENRY. It'll bounce.
PETER. Never mind, write it.
      (HENRY *moves to the sideboard and opens the cheque-book.*)
HENRY. The date?

PETER. Today.
HELEN. No, yesterday. Today's Sunday.
PETER. Yesterday then.
HENRY. Who to?
PETER (*indicating* JULIA). Her.
JULIA. Oh no!
HENRY. What name?
JULIA. J. V. Fawcett. But not for me.
HENRY. With a U?
JULIA. With a W. But I couldn't possibly take money.
HENRY (*to* PETER). How much?
PETER. Fifteen hundred.
HENRY. I see! Yes, I see.
HELEN. What a splendid idea.
HENRY (*writing*). —only—H. Hampster.

(PETER *takes the cheque as* HENRY *tears it out.*)
PETER. Fill in the counterfoil.
HENRY. Oh, yes.

(HENRY *does so while* PETER *takes the cheque across to* JULIA.)
PETER. We pay better.
JULIA. But what do you expect me to do?

(*She takes the cheque.* PETER *offers her a cigarette.*)
PETER. Cigarette?

(JULIA *stands with the cheque in one hand. Her other hand goes slowly to the cigarette. She takes it.* HELEN *comes up to her with a lighter.*
They watch as JULIA *puts the cigarette in her mouth and allows it to be lit.*
They breath a sigh of relief. HENRY *turns to the drinks.*)
HENRY. Gin, whisky, brandy?
JULIA. I don't know.
HELEN. Gin. And me, Henry.

(JULIA *looks at the cigarette.*)
JULIA. I don't like it much.
ALL (*together*). You will.

(HENRY *comes forward with a gin and tonic.*)
HENRY. And this.

(JULIA *puts the cheque into her jacket pocket and takes the glass.* HENRY *hands one to* HELEN *and turns back to the drinks and pours himself one. He turns to* PETER.)
Help yourself.

(*As* PETER *goes up to the sideboard* JULIA *takes a sip.* HELEN *watches her.*)

HELEN. I spat my first sip out.
HENRY. You weren't paid for it. (*Aside to* PETER.) Eleven hundred would have done.
PETER. Skinflint.
HENRY. Money's money.
JULIA. It's quite nice. Fizzy.
HENRY. That's the tonic. (*He raises his glass.*) Cheers. (*He drinks.*) Not nearly twelve. I've broken a lifelong rule. I feel quite guilty.
JULIA. I don't.
HELEN. Oh good, my dear, I'm so glad.
JULIA. In fact, I feel unguilty. You see, when I was sixteen I did actually smoke a cigarette, but I was drunk at the time, so it didn't count.
PETER. You've been through all this before?
JULIA. Yes, and I felt terrible about it. I've worried and worried about what I was going to say to Mummy and Daddy when I was twenty-one.
HENRY. Had you decided?
JULIA. Yes, actually. I wasn't going to say anything.
PETER. Deceitful.
JULIA. But they'd have been so disappointed. I mean, they wanted to give me the money.
HENRY. And now you've got it.
JULIA. Yes. (*She reads the cheque.*) And I can do anything I like. Oh, thank you!
(*She kisses* HENRY *impulsively.* HELEN *rises.*)
HELEN. My dear—
(*She kisses* HELEN.)
HENRY (*indicating* PETER). He's the fellow that deserves the kisses.
(*She goes up to him. He makes no move. She hesitates.*)
PETER. That cheque is only worth money if you go on deceiving the bank.
HENRY. As you did, no more, no less.
JULIA. I am sort of owed that money now.
HELEN. Of course you are!
HENRY (*to* PETER). It was your idea.
HELEN. The whole thing was. Mind you, though, I don't think you've been very enterprising.
HENRY. I wouldn't say unenterprising.
HELEN. But content to live in such a humdrum way—week in week out; you know what I mean. He hasn't developed the situation.
HENRY. Didn't have time, did you, old man? All those girls.

JULIA. That's over, anyway.

(*She holds out her glass.* HENRY *takes it and refills it.*)

PETER. Yes, that's over.
HELEN. So we can start to enjoy ourselves.
PETER. How?
HELEN. Do all the things that people do. Trips abroad, two cars.
HENRY. Why not four?
HELEN. Why not? And fun, we can have lots of fun.
PETER. What sort?
HELEN. All sorts. Don't be a wet blanket.
HENRY. We could go to Ascot, Goodwood, the Royal Tournament.
HELEN. The Edinburgh Festival!
JULIA. The Dublin Horse Show!
PETER. All together?
HELEN. Why not?
HENRY. Wimbledon—Lords, the Boat Race!

(PETER *is beginning to look hunted.*)

JULIA. Badminton!
HELEN. Motspur Park.
JULIA. What happens there?
HELEN. I don't know. Some kind of races.
JULIA. And every fourth year we could go to the Olympic Games.
PETER. You couldn't. You have to stay at the bank.
HENRY. No, she doesn't. There's a way round that. Now, let me just work it out. We don't really need nine million. I mean, a hundred thousand each would do us.
HELEN. Two hundred.
HENRY. Two hundred, then—no, say two-fifty. That makes a round million. Draw that out, split it between us and close the account.
JULIA. You can't very well close it with eight million still in it.
HELEN. And a pity, in a way.
HENRY. All right then; in for a penny, in for a pound. Two million, two hundred and fifty thousand each.
PETER. Not for me, thank you.
HENRY. Oh yes.
HELEN. Naturally.
PETER. Three into nine makes three million each. Rounder.
JULIA (*going to him*). But, darling, you wouldn't want me to be richer than you.
HENRY. And besides—
HELEN. Yes.
HENRY. You're one of us.

PETER. No.
HELEN. You must be.
HENRY. After all—
JULIA (*her arms round him*). What else could you be, darling?
PETER. What I was, what I am.
HELEN. You were a complete parasite.
JULIA. And now we're all together.
HENRY. United we stand, divided we fall.
HELEN. Besides, you'll enjoy it.
PETER. I hate races.
HELEN. Nonsense, don't be affected.
HENRY. You don't have to compete, you know; just sit around and watch.
JULIA. Or stroll about the paddock.
PETER. No, no!
HENRY. And, of course, with money it's even more fun. You can present a prize and have a race named after yourself. (*Trying it out for sound.*) "The Hampster Cup."
JULIA. The Fawcett Plate.
HENRY. The Pounce Trophy.
PETER. Oh, God!
HELEN. The Helen Hampster Prize.
HENRY. For needlework.
HELEN (*indignant*). Why should it be for needlework?
HENRY. It sounds like it. Or for English.
HELEN (*to* JULIA). Isn't that a man all over? Isn't it? Just because I'm a woman it has to be needlework. (*To* HENRY.) As though you were an athlete. You! Why you never won a race in your life.
HENRY. How do you know?
HELEN. Well, have you?
HENRY. Yes, I have.
HELEN. When?
HENRY. When I was at school. I won the sack-race.
HELEN. And you're boasting about that?
HENRY. No, no, I am not boasting, but you said never in your life, and I said yes, in my life, once at any rate. Which makes you wrong.
HELEN. Do you really think you have the right to be supercilious about women just because you once ran faster than a lot of little boys?
HENRY. I was a little boy, too.
HELEN. And even then you had to put your head in a sack to do it.
HENRY. My head in a sack?
HELEN. You said it was a sack-race.
HENRY. It was. But, Helen, my dear, in a sack-race you put your feet in the sack.

HELEN. Oh, Henry, Henry, really! Over the head; that's how it goes. (*To* JULIA.) Doesn't it?
JULIA. I'm not absolutely sure—
HELEN. Everybody knows that. What would be the point of putting your feet in it? You could see.
   (PETER *watches the argument develop with interest, an idea for escaping comes into his head.*)
HENRY (*shrugging*). One can't argue.
HELEN. You must be growing terribly old, darling, if you've forgotten what a sack-race is like.
HENRY. I remember things very well. Much better than you.
HELEN. Quite the most forgetful man I've ever met.
HENRY. Forgetful's nothing to do with remembering things.
HELEN (*appealing to the others*). Now he doesn't even know the meaning of the words.
HENRY. I do, I do! You don't, it all means the same to you. But I can distinguish, ah yes, distinguish between remembering where my toothbrush is and remembering what happened at school. They're quite, quite different things.
PETER (*nudging the argument back into line*). I took part in a sack-race at school.
HENRY. And so did I and won it, too. We climbed into the sack and we jumped along.
HELEN. What a peculiar school.
HENRY. It was a perfectly normal one.
HELEN. You hated it.
HENRY. Perhaps, but it was normal.
HELEN. So you were abnormal.
HENRY. No, no, I don't say that.
HELEN. You must have been if you put your feet in the sack.
HENRY. Look, every single other person in the school was doing it!
HELEN. And of course you had to. Oh yes, that's exactly you—always conform, run with the crowd, play safe.
HENRY. At least I didn't go to a school where everyone shoved their heads in sacks.
HELEN. I did Greek!
JULIA. Greek?
HELEN. Yes, Greek—and you always put your head in the sack. (*Appealing to the others.*) Don't you?
PETER. Yes.
HENRY (*stupefied*). What?
PETER. Yes, you do, always.
HELEN. Two to one, Henry.
HENRY. You can't do it, simply not at all; it doesn't make sense.

PETER. Try.
HENRY. All right, very well. I'll show you; yes, I will. (*He goes off quickly into the kitchen.*) You'll soon see how idiotic you are.
PETER (*to* HELEN). You show him.
HELEN. There's only one sack.
    (PETER *rips open a long cushion cover from the armchair and takes the cushion out.*)
PETER. Use this. You might have a race.
JULIA. What fun.
    (*He takes off the other cover and hands it to her.*)
PETER. And for you. Much cleaner than sacks.
JULIA. What do we do?
    (HENRY *enters, the sack already over his head. Pace or two forward.*)
HENRY (*contemptuously*). What sort of a race can you have like this? We'll just blunder round, bumping into things. (*He bumps into* HELEN.)
HELEN. Is that you?
HENRY. Yes, it is.
HELEN. Well, stand still. Peter will line us up.
HENRY. He's not competing, I notice.
PETER. I'll be the starter and the judge.
HELEN. You turn us round three times.
    (PETER *has now tied up* JULIA.)
JULIA. Are you sure you aren't thinking of Blind Man's Buff?
HENRY. That's it, that's what you were thinking of—Blind Man's Buff. You've got it all wrong. (*He cannons into a piece of furniture in his enthusiasm.*)
HELEN. Henry, stand still!
HENRY. All right, what happens now?
PETER. I say, "On your marks, get set—" (*He goes to the door.*)
HENRY. How can we get set? (*He half bends down.*)
JULIA. One—two—three—
HELEN. Yes, much better, one—two—three— Go!
    (*They are all in a line facing* D.S.)
HENRY. It was never like this when I was young.
HELEN. It was—oh, yes it was. Wasn't it, Julia?
JULIA. I am young.
HENRY. Well, tell us to go.
PETER. One.
JULIA. Where do we go?
PETER. Two—

HELEN. Straight ahead.
PETER. Three.
JULIA. No, wait, wait! I'm sure we've got it wrong.
PETER. Too late now. Go!

As they start to move forward PETER *goes out with a slam of the door. Before they fall into the orchestra pit, down comes the* CURTAIN *with a bang.*

FURNITURE AND PROPERTY PLOT

On TV set
  Two magazines

On mantelpiece
  Two glass vases
  Two china ducks
  Tobacco jar
  Pipe
  Two brass candlesticks
  Box of matches

  Wastepaper basket in grate

Settee
  Cushion with cover (press stud opening)
  Knitting D.S. end

On D.S. end coffee table
  Ashtray and book matches

On round table
  Small bowl everlasting flowers
  Table lighter
  Small ashtray

On sideboard
  Table lamp
  Tonic water
  Opener
  Tray
  Bottles gin, brandy, whisky
  Four spirit glasses
  Four sherry glasses
  Four pony glasses
  Small ashtray
  Vase (to take knitting)
  Table lighter
  Silver cigarette box
  Telephone

In centre drawer
  Four silver knives
  Four silver forks
  Two rolled bamboo mats
  White tablecloth (flimsy and wearable)
  Two other tablecloths

In cupboard
  Silver cruet
  China cruet
  Various sauces

In lower drawer
  Spare cheque book and pen

In cabinet
  Second drawer from bottom
    Personal letters
    Birth certificates
    Gas bills
    Bank statement

  Bottom drawer
    Two typewritten letters
    Several handwritten letters, all in envelopes

On bookcase
  Books
  Vase

On table
  Clock
  Vase

Off stage
Bedroom
  Two suitcases
  Cheval mirror
  Table with towel, shaving soap, brush, razor, mirror

R.
   Two Sunday papers
   Holdall containing bottle sherry (practical)
   Winebottle wrapped in tissue
   Flat brown parcel
   Small wrapped loaf
   Lemon
   Box of fifty cigarettes

L.
   Tray with coffee set
   Tray with breakfast things:
      Coffee set
      Egg
      Toast
      Butter dish
      Three plates, knives and spoons
   Tray with plate of bananas, plate of cheese and knife
   Tray with two plates lettuce and salmon, small plate brown bread

White candle
Sacks
Apron
Red tablecloth
Silver tray with teapot:
   Sugar bowl
   Milk jug
   Plate of cakes
   Small plate bread and butter
   Tray with two dirty teacups, saucers and plates, small plate sandwiches
Manuscript

Personal props

HENRY Box of 32 matches
             Cheque book
             Pen
PETER Drawing pin in shoe
JULIA Handbag

THE COPYRIGHT ACT, 1956

N.B. *Before any performance of this play can be given, application must first be made to* EVANS BROTHERS LIMITED *for a licence, and it is advisable that this should be done* **before rehearsals begin.** *Any performance of this play without a licence is illegal. For full particulars please refer to* COPYRIGHT NOTICE *on page 2 of cover.*